# An
# OVID
# Workbook

## Teacher's Manual

**LLWS**
Latin Literature Workbook Series

# A Series Edited by LeaAnn A. Osburn

*A Horace Workbook* (2005)
*A Horace Workbook Teacher's Manual* (2006)
*A Vergil Workbook* (2006)
*A Vergil Workbook Teacher's Manual* (2007)
*An Ovid Workbook* (2006)
*An Ovid Workbook Teacher's Manual* (2007)
*A Catullus Workbook* (2006)
*A Catullus Workbook Teacher's Manual* (2007)
*A Cicero Workbook* (2006)
*A Cicero Workbook Teacher's Manual* (2007)

# An OVID Workbook

## Teacher's Manual

Charbra Adams Jestin
& Phyllis B. Katz

Bolchazy-Carducci Publishers, Inc.
Wauconda, Illinois USA

*Series Editor*
LeaAnn A. Osburn

*Volume General Editor*
Donald E. Sprague

*Volume Contributing Editor*
Karrie Lee Singh, PhD

*Typography, Page and Cover Design*
Adam Phillip Velez

**An Ovid Workbook**
**Teacher's Manual**

by Charbra Adams Jestin & Phyllis B. Katz

© 2007 Bolchazy-Carducci Publishers, Inc.
All rights reserved.

**Bolchazy-Carducci Publishers, Inc.**
1000 Brown Street
Wauconda, IL 60084 USA
www.bolchazy.com

Printed in the United States of America
**2007**
by Publisher's Graphics

ISBN 978-0-86516-626-4

# CONTENTS

# FOREWORD

All Latin teachers want their students to read ancient authors in the original. Yet to study the authentic Latin of an ancient Roman author is a complex task. It requires comprehension of the text and its grammatical underpinnings; an understanding of the world events and the culture in which the work of literature was produced; an ability to recognize the figures of speech the author uses and to grasp the impact they have on the text; sensitivity to the way sound effects, including meter if a passage is poetry, interact with the meaning of the text; and the ability to probe whatever thoughts and ideas the author may be expressing. To be successful in this multifaceted task, students need not only a comprehensive textbook but also exercises of different kinds, in which to practice their newly developing literary and critical skills.

Students often need extensive drill and practice material—something not available in the traditional Latin author textbook—to help them master the grammar and syntax of the Latin text as well as the literary skills that the text demands of its readers. Teachers, too, no matter how many questions they ask in class to help their students analyze the syntax and the literary qualities of the text, often need and want more questions to be available. Realizing this need on the part of both students and teachers, Bolchazy-Carducci Publishers has begun to develop a series of workbooks to accompany Advanced Placement textbooks. There will be five workbooks in the series, one for each advanced placement author: Catullus, Cicero, Horace, Ovid, and Vergil. A team of authors—one, a university scholar with special expertise in the Latin literary text and the other, a high school Advanced Placement Latin teacher—will write each workbook.

Workbooks in this series will contain the Latin text as delineated on the Advanced Placement Syllabus and exercises that drill grammar, syntax, and figures of speech. In addition, multiple choice questions will be included and will focus on the student's comprehension of the passage and on items of literary analysis. The workbooks will also feature scansion practice, essays to write, and other short analysis questions in each section. By reading and answering these types of questions, students will gain experience with the types of questions that are found on the Advanced Placement Examinations. Students at the college level will also benefit from the additional practice offered in the workbooks.

These workbooks contain neither textual notes nor vocabulary on the page with the text nor on the facing page. The absence of these traditional features of textbooks will allow students, after reading the Latin passage in the textbook, to practice in the workbook what they have learned and to assess how much they have mastered already and what needs more study. The workbooks will, however, contain a Latin to English Vocabulary at the back of the book.

We are confident that this series of workbooks has a unique role to play in fostering students' understanding of authentic Latin text and will be a significant addition to the Advanced Placement and college materials that already exist.

LeaAnn A. Osburn
Series Editor

# PREFACE TO THE STUDENT WORKBOOK

This workbook has been designed to give students confidence in reading the poetry of Ovid with full comprehension. Students preparing for the nationally-administered Advanced Placement Latin Literature Exam in Ovid will find ample practice for that exam in this workbook. College students using this workbook will find a useful resource for their study of Ovid's poetry. The workbook can be used in conjunction with any edition of Ovid's poems. The text printed and the Latin Vocabulary included are those published in our text, *Ovid: Amores, Metamorphoses, Selections* (Wauconda, IL: Bolchazy-Carducci Publishers, 1998, Second edition, 2003).

You will find several types of questions in each chapter to help strengthen students' ability to understand the composition of Ovid's poetry and its meaning. The first part of each chapter contains questions targeting grammatical analysis of the passage at hand. Questions of this sort help to confirm that students are reading the Latin of the passage accurately.

Each chapter of the workbook also includes a second part with multiple choice questions. These test a variety of material in the passage: structure, translation, comprehension, figures of speech, scansion, and references. We have included these in this workbook as a means for students to practice and evaluate their skills in these areas. The figure of speech that is sometimes called interlocked word order is identified in this workbook by the more formal term "synthesis," which is also spelled "synchysis" in some texts. Tricolon crescendo, sometimes called tricolon crescens in other texts, is the term used in this workbook.

In the third part of each chapter in this workbook students will gain practice in rendering into literal English a six- to eight-line segment from the passage in the chapter. This exercise represents the same length selection as on the Advanced Placement exam. Students should strive for the greatest accuracy possible in the translation of these selections, and should bear in mind that accurate translation is an aid to reading Latin with fluency.

Each chapter also includes a fourth part with short response questions of the sort seen in the Identification Questions on the Advanced Placement exam or comparable college Latin exams. The questions are generally worded to lead the student to a short, rather specific answer.

For each of the *Amores* and each of the longer passages from the *Metamorphoses* you will also find a section that contains a twenty-minute essay topic. These essays should be written on a separate sheet of paper. The more practice students have in writing these essays the better they become at writing concise, yet strong essays that are based specifically on the question posed. In each essay students should provide ample reference to the Latin, properly cited, either translated or paraphrased accurately, that supports their argument. Essays should always be analytical in nature rather than a narrative, that is, students should not summarize a passage but rather construct an argument that is based on the Latin that applies to the essay question.

---

* AP is a registered trademark of the College Entrance Examination Board, which was not involved in the production of, and does not endorse, this product.

You will also find a part that gives students practice in scanning lines from the passages. *Scansion should always be a part of poetic analysis* and may add weight to an argument made in an essay.

A final supplementary part asks students to work with the vocabulary of the passage. Vocabulary building is an important part of students' preparation for reading Ovid confidently. Without a sufficient vocabulary, students stumble through translations and give weak answers. Some of the vocabulary sections ask students to search for words with a common theme, while other sections ask them to recall words and to learn words that they do not yet know. As students gain more familiarity with Ovid's vocabulary, they will understand and appreciate his poetry more fully.

Over the course of their study of the passages from the *Amores* and the *Metamorphoses*, students will be reading some wonderful literature and will come to understand the poetic voice Ovid has created for himself in his poems. We are certain that with diligence and with the help of the exercises in this workbook, students will expand and enhance their ability to enjoy and admire this author's poetry.

CHARBRA ADAMS JESTIN
Avon High School
Avon, Connecticut

PHYLLIS B. KATZ
Dartmouth College
Hanover, New Hampshire

# PREFACE TO THE TEACHER'S MANUAL

Our goal in writing this workbook has been to provide ample practice for students preparing to take the Ovid portion of the AP* Latin Literature Examination. We hope that with sufficient practice in the types of questions found on the exam, students will gain confidence in translating and comprehending the works of Ovid included in the Advanced Placement syllabus and will feel well-prepared for the examination in May.

With these goals in mind each chapter contains questions formatted specifically in the style of those found on the examination as well as some questions in alternate styles to ensure full preparation. Every chapter contains a Part I that covers grammatical constructions to confirm that students are reading passages with correct syntax, a Part II that contains multiple choice questions that will not only confirm student comprehension of the Ovid passages but will provide practice for the sight passages found in Section I on the AP* exam, a Part III that offers a standard translation passage of six to eight lines, and a Part IV that requires short responses on analysis and comprehension questions modeled directly on the short identification questions on the AP* Ovid exam. Additionally, each of the *Amores* selections as well as each selection from the *Metamorphoses* includes Parts V–VII. Part V is a twenty-minute essay question modeled on the AP* exam format, Part VI provides practice in scansion, and Part VII offers various exercises designed to help in building vocabulary. Because vocabulary review is essential for improving and reinforcing translation skills, we have included vocabulary practice for each passage. The words included in the **Vocabulary Check** exercises are all words occurring at least three times in the Ovid syllabus. Over the last several years, readers' reports coming from the AP* grading committee have stressed the need for accurately translated Latin on the exam. Teachers may adjust assignments in the vocabulary section based on the proficiency of a given class.

The longer *Metamorphoses* passages have been split into manageable sections of approximately thirty-five lines (each including Parts I–IV). A single Part V–VII is provided in the final section for each long passage. Teachers will want to tailor assignments for the long passages to suit the abilities of their classes.

This manual contains answers for all parts of the student workbook. The grammatical analysis and multiple choice answers are straightforward. The translation passages have been divided into word groupings to facilitate using the AP* nine-point scale. The short analysis questions generally have one correct answer; however, we do not want to rule out other possible interpretations. For each essay question a six-point descriptive rubric, similar to the one used by AP* graders, has been provided. For those vocabulary sections, like that for *Amores* 1.3, that present a high-frequency check list, we have not included the dictionary entries as these sections are intended as checks for the students themselves and not necessarily as class activities.

---

* AP is a registered trademark of the College Entrance Examination Board, which was not involved in the production of, and does not endorse, this product.

For full information on the Advanced Placement Latin Literature Examination, including a description of the exam, its content, teaching hints, format, scoring, and recent exams, be sure to visit the AP* Central Latin Literature Home Page at http://apcentral.collegeboard.com.

CHARBRA ADAMS JESTIN
Avon High School, Avon, Connecticut

PHYLLIS B. KATZ
Dartmouth College, Hanover, New Hampshire

# TEXT OF
# THE *AMORES*
# WITH EXERCISES
# & ANSWERS

# AMORES 1.1

Arma gravi numero violentaque bella parabam
    edere, materia conveniente modis.
par erat inferior versus; risisse Cupido
    dicitur atque unum surripuisse pedem.
5    "quis tibi, saeve puer, dedit hoc in carmina iuris?
    Pieridum vates, non tua, turba sumus.
quid si praeripiat flavae Venus arma Minervae,
    ventilet accensas flava Minerva faces?
quis probet in silvis Cererem regnare iugosis,
10    lege pharetratae virginis arva coli?
crinibus insignem quis acuta cuspide Phoebum
    instruat, Aoniam Marte movente lyram?
sunt tibi magna, puer, nimiumque potentia regna:
    cur opus affectas ambitiose novum?
15    an, quod ubique, tuum est? tua sunt Heliconia tempe?
    vix etiam Phoebo iam lyra tuta sua est?
cum bene surrexit versu nova pagina primo,
    attenuat nervos proximus ille meos.
nec mihi materia est numeris levioribus apta,
20    aut puer aut longas compta puella comas."
questus eram, pharetra cum protinus ille soluta
    legit in exitium spicula facta meum
lunavitque genu sinuosum fortiter arcum
    "quod" que "canas, vates, accipe" dixit "opus."
25    me miserum! certas habuit puer ille sagittas.
    uror, et in vacuo pectore regnat Amor.
sex mihi surgat opus numeris, in quinque residat;
    ferrea cum vestris bella valete modis.
cingere litorea flaventia tempora myrto,
30    Musa per undenos emodulanda pedes.

## Short Answer Questions

Line 1    What is the case and use of *arma* and *bella*? **accusative, direct object of *parabam***

Line 2    What is the case and use of *materia conveniente*? **ablative absolute**

Line 7    What is the tense and mood of *praeripiat*? **present subjunctive**

        What is the reason for that tense and mood? **future less vivid condition**

Line 9    What are the tense, mood, and voice of *regnare*? **present infinitive active**

What is the reason for that mood? **indirect statement (after *probet*)**

What is the case and use of *Cererem?* **accusative subject of *regnare* indirect statement**

Line 11    What is the case and use of *crinibus?* **ablative of cause/respect/specification (with *insignem*)**

Line 13    What is the case and use of *tibi?* **dative of possession**

Line 24    What is the tense and mood of *canas?* **present subjunctive**

What is the reason for that tense and mood? **relative clause of characteristic**

Line 25    What is the case and use of *me miserum?* **accusative of exclamation**

Line 29    What is the tense and mood of *cingere?* **imperative present**

What is the reason for that tense and mood? **command**

# Multiple Choice Questions *Suggested time: 12 minutes*

1.  The examples cited in lines 7–12 are to suggest

    a. **that the gods cannot have their roles reversed**

    b.  that there is rivalry among the gods

    c.  the reasons that Cupid and the poet are not alike

    d.  that Cupid is ambitious

2.  A figure of speech found in lines 7–12 is

    a.  hyperbaton

    b.  polysyndeton

    c. **tricolon crescendo**

    d.  onomatopoeia

3.  In line 8, the poet uses the figure of speech

    a.  litotes

    b.  personification

    c.  metaphor

    d. **chiasmus**

4.  In line 8, the *faces* refer to

    a.  anger

    b.  torch light

    c. **love and marriage**

    d.  rods of authority

5.  The metrical pattern for the first four feet of line 19 is

    a.  dactyl-spondee-dactyl-dactyl

    b. **dactyl-dactyl-dactyl-dactyl**

    c.  spondee-spondee-dactyl-spondee

    d.  dactyl-dactyl-spondee-dactyl

6.  The case of *longas comas* (line 20) is governed by

    a.  *puella*

    b.  *materia*

    c.  *puer*

    d. **compta**

7. In line 21, the case and number of *pharetra* are
   - a. nominative singular
   - b. nominative plural
   - **c. ablative singular**
   - d. accusative plural

8. In lines 19–20, the poet tells us
   - **a. that he is not in love**
   - b. that he has a girl friend
   - c. that he has a boy friend
   - d. that he is unhappy

9. Lines 27–28 tell us that
   - a. the poet will continue to write epic poetry
   - b. the poet cannot write elegiac (love) poetry
   - **c. the poet will now write elegiac poetry**
   - d. love poetry is full of harsh wars

10. In line 30, the case and number of *emodulanda* are
    - a. ablative singular
    - **b. nominative plural**
    - c. vocative singular
    - d. nominative singular

## Translation *Suggested time: 15 minutes*

Translate the passage below as literally as possible.

> sunt tibi magna, puer, nimiumque potentia regna:
>    cur opus affectas ambitiose novum?
> an, quod ubique, tuum est? tua sunt Heliconia tempe?
>    vix etiam Phoebo iam lyra tuta sua est?
> 5   cum bene surrexit versu nova pagina primo,
>    attenuat nervos proximus ille meos.
> nec mihi materia est numeris levioribus apta,
>    aut puer aut longas compta puella comas.

*Amores 1.1.13–20*

"You, young boy, have great and exceedingly powerful kingdoms. Why do you, ambitious one, aspire to a new job? Or, rather, is everything everywhere yours? Are the Heliconian valleys yours? Likewise, is his lyre hardly safe for Phoebus now? When a new page has risen up well in the first verse, that next [verse] weakens my strings."

**18 chunks. 9 points total, 1/2 point each. Round up to nearest whole point.**

| | |
|---|---|
| *sunt tibi* | **you have/there are to you** |
| *puer ambitiose* | **ambitious boy/ambitious one (*may be taken together or separately with each clause*)** |
| *magna nimiumque potentia regna* | **great and exceedingly powerful kingdoms** |
| *cur affectas* | **why do you aspire/attempt** |
| *opus novum* | **a new undertaking/job** |
| *an quod ubique* | **or/rather, everything everywhere/that which (is) everywhere** |

| | |
|---|---|
| *tuum est* | **is yours?** |
| *tua sunt Heliconia tempe* | **Are the Heliconian valleys yours?** |
| *vix* | **scarcely/hardly** |
| *etiam Phoebo* | **even for Phoebus** |
| *iam lyra sua* | **his lyre now** |
| *tuta est* | **is safe** |
| *cum nova pagina* | **when a new page** |
| *bene surrexit* | **has risen up well** |
| *versu primo* | **in the first verse** |
| *proximus ille* | **that next one/verse** |
| *attenuat* | **weakens/enfeebles/lessens** |
| *nervos meos* | **my strings** |

## Short Analysis Questions

1. a. Translate *saeve puer* (line 5).

   **cruel boy**

   b. When the poet calls Cupid *"saeve"* here, what figure of speech is he employing?

   **prolepsis**

2. In lines 13–14, the poet describes Cupid's sphere of influence.

   a. What figure of speech does he employ here?

   **metaphor. (The poet says that Cupid has great and too powerful kingdoms.)**

   b. Write out the exact Latin words that express the figure of speech.

   **The words *magna, nimiumque potentia regna* compare Cupid to kings and rulers.**

3. a. Exactly what is the poet describing in lines 17–18?

   **The poet is describing the damaging effect of Cupid's theft of one foot from his hexameter line.**

   b. Write out a literal translation for these lines.

   **When a new page has risen up well in the first verse, that next verse weakens my strings.**

4. a. To what muse does the poet refer in lines 29–30?

   **Erato, muse of lyric love poetry.**

   b. Write out and translate the Latin words that help to identify this muse.

   **Litorea . . . myrto, the myrtle tree of the seashore suggests Erato because the myrtle is associated with Venus, the goddess of erotic love. Or, *undenos pedes*, eleven feet, suggest Erato because there are eleven feet in an elegiac couplet, the traditional meter of elegiac love poetry.**

# Essay *Suggested time: 20 minutes*

In *Amores* 1.1, the poet describes himself as tricked and/or forced by Cupid to renounce the writing of epic poetry and instead become a love poet. Write an essay in which you discuss the nature of the love god's trick and the poet's response to it. Consider the tone established by this poem as an introduction to three books of love poetry.

Support your assertions with references drawn from **throughout** the poem. All Latin words must be copied or their line numbers provided, AND they must be translated or paraphrased closely enough so that it is clear you understand the Latin. It is your responsibility to convince your reader that you are basing your conclusions on the Latin text and not merely on a general recollection of the passage. Direct your answer to the question; do not merely summarize the passage. Please write your essay on a separate piece of paper.

**The question asks the student to evaluate the introductory poem of the *Amores* in terms of its content and tone. Students should think about how and why the poet describes himself as tricked by Cupid and how he responds to the love god's trick, looking closely at the speaker's arguments. They should discuss the speaker's conversation about Cupid's theft of one foot from each second line of his poetry, paying close attention to the speaker's major argument (lines 7–12), as well as his definition of Cupid's allotted territory (lines 13–16). They should also note the speaker's final argument (lines 19–20) and Cupid's response to it (lines 21–24), bearing in mind throughout that this poem sets the scene for the entire three books of the *Amores*. The grader of this essay should look for an argument that considers how the trick and the conversation and actions that surround it result in a tone that is both humorous and "tongue in cheek."**

**6 – A fully-developed essay which shows how Ovid develops the speaker's explanation of his switch from epic to elegiac poetry through the device of a trick played on the speaker by Cupid. The analysis looks at how the speaker's description of his own duping and transformation serves as an ironic explanation of why he is writing love poetry. The student uses the Latin text fully and accurately to support his arguments. In spite of some occasional mistakes, the essay is coherent and well-developed.**

**5 – A strong essay, but not fully developed or fully supported by the text. The essay shows a good understanding of the poem, and cites the Latin correctly, but does not go far enough in showing the irony in the speaker's explanations.**

**4 – A good essay, but one that does not reveal a real understanding the function of irony and humor in a poem that serves as an introduction to a collection of love poetry. The writer may describe the arguments in the poem without showing their function. Citation of the passage is spotty and the Latin support is not extensive.**

**3 – A weak essay. The Latin citations are inappropriate and poorly cited; there is little or no analysis of the passage. Or, the student shows perception of the meaning of the passage, but does not cite Latin to support his points.**

**2 – A general, non-focused essay. There is no coherent discussion and the Latin passages are not accurate or appropriate.**

**1** – A response that lacks coherence and has no central argument. The essay does not demonstrate an understanding of the poem.

**0** – The response is irrelevant to the topic or incorrect, or merely restates the question without any analysis.

# Scansion

Scan the following lines.

>    ‒   ∪ ∪ ‒ ∪ ∪ ‒ ∪∪ ‒   ∪ ∪   ‒ ∪ ∪ ‒ ‒
> **Arma gravi numero violentaque bella parabam**

>     ‒ ∪∪   ‒ ∪∪ ‒   ‒   ∪ ∪ ‒ ∪ ∪ ‒
> **edere, materia conveniente modis.**

>    ‒   ∪∪ ‒  ∪∪ ‒   ‒ ‒   ‒ ‒ ∪ ∪ ‒ ‒
> **par erat inferior versus; risisse Cupido**

>     ‒∪∪ ‒   ‒ ‒   ‒ ∪ ∪ ‒ ∪ ∪ ‒
> **dicitur atqu(e) unum surripuisse pedem.**

*Amores 1.1.1–4*

# Vocabulary

The vocabulary exercises require you to provide the dictionary entry for a given Latin word. List nouns by nominative and genitive singular and gender; list adjectives by all nominative singular forms; list verbs by principal parts. In this exercise, also provide the principal meaning for each word. Use the blanks provided for your list. Provide line references in parentheses beside your Latin choices.

1. List ten Latin words in the poem that refer to weapons or war.

   a. *arma, -orum* **(n.pl.) weapons (line 1)**

   b. *bellum, -i* **(n.) war (line 1)**

   c. *turba, -ae* **(f.) troop (line 6)**

   d. *pharetratus, -a, -um* **furnished with a quiver (line 10)**

   e. *cuspis, -idis* **(f.) spear (line 11)**

   f. *instruo, -ere, -xi, -ctum* **to equip, arrange, furnish (line 12)**

   g. *nervus, -i* **(m.) string of musical instrument or of a bow (line 18)**

   h. *pharetra, -ae* **(f.) quiver (line 21)**

i.   *spiculum, -i* (n.) arrow (line 22)

j.   *arcus, -i* (m.) bow (line 23)
     OR
     *sagitta, -ae* (f.) arrow (line 25)

2.  List the names of nine gods or goddesses in the poem.

a.  *Cupido, -inis* (m.) Cupid (god of love) (line 3)

b.  *Pierides, -um* (f. pl.) the muses (line 6)

c.  *Venus, -eris* (f.) Venus (goddess of love) (line 7)

d.  *Minerva, -ae* (f.) Minerva (goddess of wisdom, war) (line 8)

e.  *Ceres, -eris* (f.) Ceres (goddess of crops and fields) (line 9)

f.  *Phoebus, -i* (m.) Phoebus Apollo (god of music and poetry) (line 11)

g.  *Mars, Martis* (m.) Mars (god of war) (line 12)

h.  *Amor, -oris* (m.) god of love, Cupid (line 26)

i.  *Musa, -ae* (f.) a muse (one of the nine) (line 30)

3.  List five words for parts of the body.

a.  *crinis, -is* (m.) hair (line 11)

b.  *coma, -ae* (f. ) hair (line 20)

c.  *genu, us* (n.) knee (line 23)

d.  *pectus, -oris* (n.) breast (line 26)

e.  *tempus, -oris* (n.) temple/forehead (line 29)

4.  List nine words that refer to poetry or poetic meter.

a.  *numerus, -i* (m.) number, meter (line 1)

b.  *versus, -i* (m.) verse (line 3)

c.  *carmen, -inis* (n.) song, poem (line 5)

d.  *vates, vatis* (m.) prophetic poet (line 6)

e.  *opus, eris* (n.) work (line 14)

f.  *lyra, -ae* (f.) lyre, lute (instrument used to accompany poetry) (line 16)

g.  *cano, canere, cecini, cantum* sing (write poetry) (line 24)

h.  *modus, -i* (m.) meter (line 28)

i.  *pes, pedis* (m.) foot (of a poetic line) (line 30)

5. List two proper nouns or adjectives that refer to geographic locations.

   a. *Aonia, -ae* (f.) Boetia (line 12)

   b. *Heliconius, -a, um* pertaining to Mt. Helicon (line 15)

# AMORES 1.3

Iusta precor: quae me nuper praedata puella est,
    aut amet aut faciat, cur ego semper amem.
a, nimium volui: tantum patiatur amari,
    audierit nostras tot Cytherea preces.
5    accipe, per longos tibi qui deserviat annos;
    accipe, qui pura norit amare fide.
si me non veterum commendant magna parentum
    nomina, si nostri sanguinis auctor eques,
nec meus innumeris renovatur campus aratris,
10    temperat et sumptus parcus uterque parens,
at Phoebus comitesque novem vitisque repertor
    hac faciunt et me qui tibi donat Amor
et nulli cessura fides, sine crimine mores,
    nudaque simplicitas purpureusque pudor.
15    non mihi mille placent, non sum desultor amoris:
    tu mihi, si qua fides, cura perennis eris;
tecum, quos dederint annos mihi fila sororum,
    vivere contingat teque dolente mori;
te mihi materiem felicem in carmina praebe:
20    provenient causa carmina digna sua.
carmine nomen habent exterrita cornibus Io
    et quam fluminea lusit adulter ave
quaeque super pontum simulato vecta iuvenco
    virginea tenuit cornua vara manu.
25    nos quoque per totum pariter cantabimur orbem
    iunctaque semper erunt nomina nostra tuis.

## Short Answer Questions

Line 1    List all the verbs governed by the subject *puella*. **praedata est (line 1), amet (line 2), faciat (line 2), patiatur (line 3)**

Line 2    Translate *amet*. **"let her love"**

    Translate *faciat*. **"let her reveal"**

Line 3    Translate *patiatur*. **"let her allow"**

    What type of infinitive is *amari* and how is it best translated? **present passive; "to be loved"**

Line 6    What is the case and use of *fide*? **ablative of manner**

Line 12      What is the antecedent of *qui?* **Amor**

Line 13      What is the case and use of *nulli?* **dative, indirect object of *cessura***

From which verb is *cessura* formed? **cedo, cedere, cessi, cessum**

What type of participle is it? **future active**

How is it best translated? **"(which) will yield/yielding/about to yield"**

Line 16      What is the case and use of *perennis?* **predicate nominative**

Line 17      What is the subject of *dederint?* **fila (line 17)**

Line 18      What is the case and use of *teque dolente?* **ablative absolute**

Translate this phrase. **"with you grieving/while you grieve"**

Line 21      What is unusual about Ovid's use of the ablative of *carmine?* **It is an ablative of place where lacking the customary preposition *in*.**

Line 24      Which noun does the adjective *virginea* modify? **manu**

Which noun does *vara* modify? **cornua**

# Multiple Choice Questions *Suggested time: 10 minutes*

1.  The antecedent of *quae* (line 1) is
    a.  *iusta*
    b.  *praedata*
    **c.  puella**
    d.  *me*

2.  In line 8, what word is missing to make the line syntactically complete?
    a.  *sum*
    b.  *sunt*
    **c.  est**
    d.  *sumus*

3.  In line 10, we learn that the author's parents are
    a.  wealthy
    **b.  frugal**
    c.  old
    d.  farmers

4.  In lines 7–10, Ovid tries to
    **a.  impress his *puella***
    b.  dissuade his *puella*
    c.  be modest
    d.  attack his *puella*

5.  In line 12, what does *Amor* give to the young girl?
    a.  the Muses
    b.  Bacchus
    **c.  Ovid**
    d.  Apollo

6. In line 14, we find an example of

    a. allegory                                  **b. alliteration**

    c. chiasmus                                 d. anaphora

7. In line 20, the poet promises his girlfriend that

    **a. he will write poems worthy of her**         b. he will pursue her forever in poetry

    c. they will sing the same worthy song         d. their cause will be worthy of this song

8. The metrical pattern of the first four feet of line 23 is

    a. dactyl-dactyl-dactyl-spondee         b. dactyl-spondee-dactyl-dactyl

    c. dactyl-spondee-spondee-spondee       **d. dactyl-spondee-dactyl-spondee**

## Translation *Suggested time: 15 minutes*

Translate the passage below as literally as possible.

> si me non veterum commendant magna parentum
>    nomina, si nostri sanguinis auctor eques,
> nec meus innumeris renovatur campus aratris,
>    temperat et sumptus parcus uterque parens,
> 5   at Phoebus comitesque novem vitisque repertor
>    hac faciunt et me qui tibi donat Amor
> et nulli cessura fides, sine crimine mores,
>    nudaque simplicitas purpureusque pudor.
>
> Amores 1.3.7–14

**If the great names of ancestors of old do not make me attractive, if the founder of my bloodline is of equestrian rank, and my field is not renewed by countless plows, and each frugal parent moderates my expenses, yet Phoebus and his nine companions, and the discoverer of the grapevine are on my side, and Love who gives me to you, and faithfulness which will yield to no one, morals without reproach, simple frankness, and blushing modesty [are on my side too].**

**18 chunks. 9 points total, 1/2 point each. Round up to nearest whole point.**

| | |
|---|---|
| *Si ... magna ... nomina* | **if great names** |
| *veterum ... parentum* | **of ancestors of old** |
| *me non ... commendant* | **do not recommend me/make me attractive** |
| *si ... auctor* | **if the founder** |
| *nostri sanguinis* | **of my bloodline** |
| *eques* [est] | **[is] of equestrian rank/is an equestrian** |
| *meus ... campus* | **and my field** |
| *nec renovatur* | **is not renewed** |
| *innumeris ... aratris* | **by countless plows** |

| | |
|---|---|
| *et ... parcus uterque parens* | and each frugal parent |
| *temperat ... sumptus* | moderates my expenses |
| *at Phoebus comitesque novem* | yet Phoebus and his nine companions |
| *vitisque repertor* | and the discoverer of the grapevine |
| *hac faciunt* | act on my behalf/are on my side |
| *et me qui tibi donat Amor* | and/as well as Love who gives me to you |
| *et nulli cessura fides* | and faithfulness which will yield to/is going to yield to no one |
| *sine crimine mores* | morals/character without reproach/blame |
| *nudaque simplicitas purpureusque pudor* | and open/simple frankness and blushing modesty |

## Short Analysis Questions

1. Why is *Cytherea* (line 4) an appropriate reference to use in this poem?

   **Cytherea is a reference to Venus, the goddess of love, who was reputedly born on the island of Cythera.**

2. Briefly discuss the effect of the concession of *si qua fides* in line 16.

   **After his strong declarations of love and the examples he so adamantly employs to highlight his love, Ovid then adds a rather crude reference to a circus rider who leaps form horse to horse suggesting a lover who leaps from bed to bed or lover to lover. Why make mention of this only to deny it? The mere mention of such plants the seed of doubt into the reader's mind as to whether or not we can trust his denial. Furthermore in the next line Ovid adds the concessive phrase, *si qua fides,* which hints that perhaps we cannot believe all he has just declared to us.**

3. To whom does Ovid refer in line 22 (*et quam . . . ave*)?

   **Leda**

4. To whom does Ovid refer in lines 23–24 (*quaeque . . . manu*)?

   **Europa**

5. Briefly discuss the relationship between the significant figure of speech and the literal meaning of line 24.

   **The maiden Europa clearly would have had difficulty grasping the horns of the moving bull as she rode astride its back. To represent this, Ovid employs a graphic chiasmus here to separate the adjective *virginea* from its noun *manu* just as the shifting horn would have moved away from the hands of the maiden.**

# Essay *Suggested time: 20 minutes*

In this poem, Ovid tries to persuade his new girlfriend to love him. In his defense he lists many examples of lovers from the world of mythology. Write an essay in which you discuss the effectiveness of these famous lovers on the poet's argument.

Support your assertions with references drawn from **throughout** the poem. All Latin words must be copied or their line numbers provided, AND they must be translated or paraphrased closely enough so that it is clear you understand the Latin. It is your responsibility to convince your reader that you are basing your conclusions on the Latin text and not merely on a general recollection of the passage. Direct your answer to the question; do not merely summarize the passage. Please write your essay on a separate piece of paper.

**The question asks the student to consider the arguments that the speaker offers to his girlfriend in support of his assertion that he will be eternally faithful to her and that he immortalize her through his poetry. Students first note those sections of the poem in which the speaker protests his faithfulness (lines 5–6) and (lines 13–15) and should then look at the three examples the speaker offers in support of his statement (19–20) that he will immortalize his beloved in his poetry. Students should point out that Io, Leda, and Europa (lines 21–24) were, in fact, deceived and raped by Jupiter. The grader should look for an essay that demonstrates awareness of the dichotomy between the speaker's protestations of eternal faithfulness and the examples that he provides.**

## Scoring Guidelines

**6 – A fully-developed essay that recognizes the hollowness of the speaker's protestations of eternal faith. The analysis looks both at the arguments that the speaker makes about his steadfast loyalty and the examples he provides to support his claims. The student uses the Latin text effectively to support his argument. The discussion is focused and convincing; there are only a very few minor inaccuracies.**

**5 – A strong essay, but not fully developed. The writer acknowledges the contrast between the speaker's assertions of faithfulness and the examples that undermine them. The Latin is accurately cited, but the discussion of the examples is weak.**

**4 – A fairly strong essay, but one that does not develop the dichotomy fully. Some accurate citations are provided as examples but the writer does not show how the examples counterbalance the rest of the poem.**

**3 – A weak response that has no central argument, one that chooses inappropriate Latin support and that does not cite the references properly. The essay is descriptive rather than analytical.**

**2 – A vague essay that shows little understanding of the question and develops no argument. The Latin chosen as examples suggests a lack of comprehension of the passages.**

**1 – A disorganized essay with no real thesis. Even though the writer uses some pertinent information from the poem, there is little or no understanding of the poem as a whole.**

**0 – A response that has nothing to do with the question and offers no relevant points. If the student simply restates the question, the essay is also given a 0.**

# Scansion

Scan the following lines.

$$\text{— — — ∪∪ — — — ∪∪ — ∪ ∪ — —}$$
**tecum, quos dederint annos mihi fila sororum,**

$$\text{— ∪∪ — — — — ∪ — ∪ — ∪ ∪—}$$
**vivere contingat teque dolente mori;**

$$\text{— ∪∪ —∪∪ — — — — ∪ ∪ — —}$$
**te mihi materiem felic(em) in carmina praebe:**

$$\text{— ∪∪— — — — ∪∪ — ∪ ∪—}$$
**provenient causa carmina digna sua.**

*Amores 1.3.17–20*

# Vocabulary

Below is a list of high frequency words you have already encountered in *Amores* 1.1 and 1.3. For all the words you know, write out full dictionary entries, including English meanings, and put a √ mark in the left-hand column to show you have already committed these words to memory. For any words you do not yet know, write out the dictionary entries using the end glossary and learn them as soon as possible.

√

1. ____ *accipiō* _____

2. ____ *amō* _____

3. ____ *amor* _____

4. ____ *aut* _____

5. ____ *carmen* _____

6. ____ *dō* _____

7. ____ *ego* _____

8. ____ *et* _____

9. ____ *faciō* _____

10. ____ *habeō* _____

11. ____ *hic* (adjective/pronoun) _____

12. ____ *longus* _____

13. _____ *magnus* _____

14. _____ *meus* _____

15. _____ *nec* _____

16. _____ *nimium* _____

17. _____ *per* _____

18. _____ *Phoebus* _____

19. _____ *puella* _____

20. _____ *quī* _____

21. _____ *sī* _____

22. _____ *sum* _____

23. _____ *suus* _____

24. _____ *tū* _____

25. _____ *vīvō* _____

# AMORES 1.9

Militat omnis amans, et habet sua castra Cupido;
    Attice, crede mihi, militat omnis amans.
quae bello est habilis, Veneri quoque convenit aetas:
    turpe senex miles, turpe senilis amor.
5  quos petiere duces animos in milite forti,
    hos petit in socio bella puella viro:
pervigilant ambo, terra requiescit uterque;
    ille fores dominae servat, at ille ducis.
  militis officium longa est via: mitte puellam,
10    strenuus exempto fine sequetur amans;
ibit in adversos montes duplicataque nimbo
    flumina, congestas exteret ille nives,
nec freta pressurus tumidos causabitur Euros
    aptave verrendis sidera quaeret aquis.
15  quis nisi vel miles vel amans et frigora noctis
    et denso mixtas perferet imbre nives?
mittitur infestos alter speculator in hostes,
    in rivale oculos alter, ut hoste, tenet.
ille graves urbes, hic durae limen amicae
20    obsidet; hic portas frangit, at ille fores.
saepe soporatos invadere profuit hostes
    caedere et armata vulgus inerme manu.
sic fera Threicii ceciderunt agmina Rhesi,
    et dominum capti deseruistis equi.
25  nempe maritorum somnis utuntur amantes
    et sua sopitis hostibus arma movent.
custodum transire manus vigilumque catervas
    militis et miseri semper amantis opus.
Mars dubius, nec certa Venus: victique resurgunt,
30    quosque neges umquam posse iacere, cadunt.
ergo desidiam quicumque vocabat amorem,
    desinat: ingenii est experientis Amor.
ardet in abducta Briseide magnus Achilles
    (dum licet, Argeas frangite, Troes, opes);
35  Hector ab Andromaches complexibus ibat ad arma,
    et galeam capiti quae daret, uxor erat;
summa ducum, Atrides visa Priameide fertur
    Maenadis effusis obstipuisse comis.
Mars quoque deprensus fabrilia vincula sensit:
40    notior in caelo fabula nulla fuit.
ipse ego segnis eram discinctaque in otia natus;
    mollierant animos lectus et umbra meos;

impulit ignavum formosae cura puellae,
iussit et in castris aera merere suis.
45       inde vides agilem nocturnaque bella gerentem:
qui nolet fieri desidiosus, amet.

# Short Answer Questions

Line 3        What is the gender, case, and number of *quae*? **feminine nominative singular**

                Which other word in this line is its antecedent? **aetas**

Line 5        Which word is the subject of *petiere*? **duces**

Line 8        What is the case and number of *ducis*? **genitive singular**

                On which other noun in the line does it depend? **fores**

Line 10      Translate *exempto fine*. **"with the end having been taken away/since the end has been taken away"**

Line 11      What is the subject of *ibit*? **"he" or "the lover" or *amans* (line 10)**

Line 13      What is the case and use of *Euros*? **accusative, direct object (of *causabitur*, deponent)**

                What type of participle is *pressurus*? **future active**

                Why is it nominative masculine singular? **It modifies the understood subject "he" or the *amans* (line 10).**

                How might it best be translated? **"about to push on"**

Line 18      What is the case and use of *hoste*? **ablative, second object of *in***

Line 30      What is the subject of *cadunt*? **an understood *ei* (functions as the antecedent to *quosque*—"those whom")**

Line 45      What type of participle is *gerentem*? **present active**

                Why is it accusative singular? **It modifies a missing direct object *me*.**

                How might it best be translated? **"waging"**

# Multiple Choice Questions *Suggested time: 13 minutes*

1.   In line 3, Ovid is making reference to

    **a.  young men**               b.  young women

    c.  mature men             d.  mature women

2. What is the figure of speech in line 3?
   a. polysyndeton
   b. antithesis
   c. **prolepsis**
   d. zeugma

3. What is the antecedent of *ille* (line 12)?
   a. *nives* (line 12)
   b. ***amans* (line 10)**
   c. *nimbo* (line 11)
   d. *Euros* (line 13)

4. In lines 13–14, Ovid employs examples drawn primarily from
   a. **sailing**
   b. marching
   c. mountain climbing
   d. drinking

5. The metrical pattern of the first four feet of line 15 is
   a. **dactyl-spondee-dactyl-spondee**
   b. spondee-dactyl-spondee-dactyl
   c. dactyl-dactyl-dactyl-spondee
   d. dactyl-spondee-spondee-spondee

6. In line 22, to whom does *vulgus* refer?
   a. girl
   b. Cupid
   c. lover
   d. **enemy**

7. What is the best translation for *visa Priameide* (line 37)?
   a. **when Cassandra had been seen**
   b. when Cassandra saw
   c. having been seen by Cassandra
   d. with Cassandra having seen him

8. What is the case and number of *fabrilia vincula* (line 39)?
   a. ablative singular
   b. nominative plural
   c. **accusative plural**
   d. nominative singular

9. In line 44, *suis* refers to
   a. Cupid
   b. Ovid
   c. the lover
   d. ***cura* (line 43)**

10. What type of subjunctive clause is *nolet* (line 46)?
    a. indirect question
    b. subjunctive by attraction
    c. **relative clause of characteristic**
    d. indirect command

11. The majority of examples Ovid offers to support his thesis come from
    a. **the Trojan War**
    b. mythology
    c. Roman love poetry
    d. the history of Rome

# Translation *Suggested time: 15 minutes*

Translate the passage below as literally as possible.

> Militat omnis amans, et habet sua castra Cupido;
>   Attice, crede mihi, militat omnis amans.
> quae bello est habilis, Veneri quoque convenit aetas:
>   turpe senex miles, turpe senilis amor.
> 5   quos petiere duces animos in milite forti,
>   hos petit in socio bella puella viro:
> pervigilant ambo, terra requiescit uterque;
>   ille fores dominae servat, at ille ducis.

*Amores 1.9.1–8*

Every lover is a soldier, and Cupid has his own camp; Atticus, believe me, every lover is a soldier. The age that is suitable for war is also suitable for love: an old soldier is a shameful thing, an old love is repulsive. The courage that generals looked for in a brave soldier a beautiful girl looks for in a companionable man. The two keep watch all night, each rests on the ground; the one guards his mistress's doors, but the other his general's.

**18 chunks. 9 points total, 1/2 point each. Round up to nearest whole point.**

| | |
|---|---|
| *Militat omnis amans* | **every/each lover is a soldier** |
| *et habet sua castra Cupido* | **and Cupid has his own camp** |
| *Attice, crede mihi* | **Atticus, believe me/trust me** |
| *militat omnis amans* | **every/each lover is a soldier** |
| *quae ... aetas* | **the age that** |
| *bello est habilis* | **is suitable/fit for war** |
| *Veneri quoque convenit* | **also is suited for love/Venus** |
| *turpe senex miles* | **an old soldier is a shameful/repulsive thing** |
| *turpe senilis amor* | **an old love is a shameful/repulsive thing** |
| *quos ... animos* | **the spirits/courage/morale [that]** |
| *petiere duces* | **leaders/generals sought out/looked for** |
| *in milite forti* | **in a strong/brave soldier** |
| *hos petit ... bella puella* | **these a beautiful girl seeks out/looks for** |
| *in socio ... viro* | **in a companionable man/husband** |
| *pervigilant ambo* | **both/the two keep watch all night** |
| *terra requiescit uterque* | **each one rests on the ground** |
| *ille fores dominae servat* | **the one guards the doors of his mistress** |
| *at ille ducis* | **but the other one his general's/leader's** |

# Short Analysis Questions

1. In lines 9–16, Ovid makes many references to storms and bad weather. Write out and translate two words or phrases that represent adverse conditions. Provide line references in parentheses for your Latin choices.

   a. *duplicataque nimbo flumina*—"rivers doubled in size by a rainstorm" (lines 11–12)

   b. *congestas nives*—"piled up snow" (line 12)
   **OR**
   *tumidos Euros*—"swelling east wind" (line 13)

2. In line 29, Ovid makes reference to *Mars* and *Venus*. Briefly explain why these two gods are significant in this context.

   **Mars, being a god of war, is a link to the soldier theme of the poem and Venus, goddess most associated with love, recalls the poem's theme of the lover.**

3. Name four heroes of the Trojan War whom Ovid mentions in this poem and briefly explain their relevance to Ovid's argument.

   a. **Rhesus, who fought on the side of the Trojans, lost his men and his famous white chariot horses as he slept, just as Ovid imagines many a lover might take his prey away from a sleeping husband.**

   b. **Achilles laments the loss of his stolen lover, Briseis, proving that even the fiercest of warriors can be a lover.**

   c. **Hector, also a great war hero, goes off to war from the embrace of his loving wife.**

   d. **Atrides (Agamemnon) is smitten by the allure of Cassandra and even risks death to preserve his love for her.**

4. a. In line 45, *nocturna bella* represents what figure of speech?

   **metaphor**

   b. To what is Ovid referring with these words?

   **This metaphor stands for the theme of this entire book of poems: lovemaking.**

# Essay *Suggested time: 20 minutes*

In traditional love poetry, Love/Venus is most frequently contrasted with War/Mars, not compared, as Ovid does in *Amores* 1.9. In a short essay, show how Ovid successfully employs these two deities as similar, not differing, in their purposes, and thus reinforces his theme that every lover is a soldier.

Support your assertions with references drawn from **throughout** the poem. All Latin words must be copied or their line numbers provided, AND they must be translated or paraphrased closely enough so that it is clear you understand the Latin. It is your responsibility to convince your reader that you are basing your conclusions on the Latin text and not merely on a general recollection of the passage. Direct your answer to the question; do not merely summarize the passage. Please write your essay on a separate piece of paper.

**The question asks the student to look closely at how and why the speaker presents Venus and Mars as similar, an assertion that the speaker first makes in line 3 in order to demonstrate that he himself has ironically become a warrior lover (lines 41–46) and hence a man of action rather than one of indolence. The student should discuss the various ways in which the speaker shows the lover and the soldier as one in purpose (lines 4–28) and may wish to include the mythological examples as well, especially (lines 39–40). The grader should look for analysis, not pure description, and at how the Latin is used as evidence**

**6 – A well-argued, coherent essay that shows both the way the speaker makes Mars and Venus equivalent, and why he does so. The analysis is supported by well-chosen examples, whose relevance is made clear. The Latin passages are cited accurately. Only a few minor errors present.**

**5 – A strong essay, but not as well supported as a 6 paper. The argument is coherent but the examples are a little thin. The writer shows familiarity with the entire poem.**

**4 – A satisfactory response, though the argument depends more on the "how" of the question than on the "why." The essay is more descriptive than analytical; important examples are omitted.**

**3 – An incomplete response with inaccurate or inappropriate citations from the Latin. Or, the student shows good understanding of the question but offers no Latin citations in support of his argument.**

**2 – A very general essay with no real focus on the question. The student fails to comprehend the cited Latin.**

**1 – A response that has no coherence and presents no real argument. The student does not show a real understanding of the poem.**

**0 – The response is irrelevant to the topic or incorrect, or merely restates the question without any analysis.**

Scan the following lines.

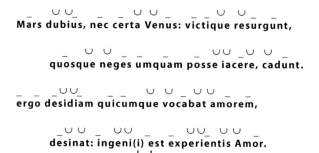

*Amores 1.9.29–32*

# Vocabulary

Below you will find a list of high frequency words you have encountered in your recent readings. For all the words you know, write out full dictionary entries, including English meanings, and put a √ mark in the left-hand column to show you have already committed these words to memory. For any words you do not yet know, write out the dictionary entries using the end glossary and learn them as soon as possible.

√

1. ____ *ā, ab* _____

2. ____ *ad* _____

3. ____ *aptus* _____

4. ____ *arma* _____

5. ____ *at* _____

6. ____ *bellum* _____

7. ____ *certus* _____

8. ____ *coma* _____

9. ____ *crinis* _____

10. ____ *Cupīdō* _____

11. ____ *dēserviō* _____

12. ____ *gravis* _____

13. ____ *ille* _____

14. ____ *in* _____

15. ____ *manus* _____

16. ____ *Mars* _____

17. ____ *miser* _____

18. ____ *moveō* _____

19. ____ *nullus* _____

20. ____ *opus* _____

21. ____ *quis* _____

22. ____ *quoque* _____

23. ____ *semper* _____

24. ____ *teneō* _____

25. ____ *uterque* _____

26. ____ *Venus* _____

# AMORES 1.11

Colligere incertos et in ordine ponere crines
    docta neque ancillas inter habenda Nape
inque ministeriis furtivae cognita noctis
    utilis et dandis ingeniosa notis,
5   saepe venire ad me dubitantem hortata Corinnam,
    saepe laboranti fida reperta mihi,
accipe et ad dominam peraratas mane tabellas
    perfer et obstantes sedula pelle moras.
nec silicum venae nec durum in pectore ferrum
10   nec tibi simplicitas ordine maior adest;
credibile est et te sensisse Cupidinis arcus:
    in me militiae signa tuere tuae.
si quaeret quid agam, spe noctis vivere dices;
    cetera fert blanda cera notata manu.
15   dum loquor, hora fugit: vacuae bene redde tabellas,
    verum continuo fac tamen illa legat.
aspicias oculos mando frontemque legentis:
    et tacito vultu scire futura licet.
nec mora, perlectis rescribat multa iubeto:
20   odi, cum late splendida cera vacat.
comprimat ordinibus versus, oculosque moretur
    margine in extremo littera †rasat† meos.
quid digitos opus est graphio lassare tenendo?
    hoc habeat scriptum tota tabella "veni."
25   non ego victrices lauro redimire tabellas
    nec Veneris media ponere in aede morer.
subscribam VENERI FIDAS SIBI NASO MINISTRAS
    DEDICAT. AT NUPER VILE FUISTIS ACER.

## Short Answer Questions

| | | |
|---|---|---|
| Line 4 | What verb form is *dandis?* | **future passive participle** |
| | What noun does it modify? | **notis** |
| Line 5 | What verb form is *dubitantem?* | **present active participle** |
| | What noun does it modify? | **Corinnam** |
| Line 6 | What is the case and use of *laboranti?* | **dative with certain adjectives (fida)** |

Lines 1–6     What are all the adjectives in these lines that modify Nape? Provide the English and line references in parentheses for your Latin choices. **docta (skilled) (line 2), habenda (to be held) (line 2), cognita (known) (line 3), utilis (useful) (line 4), ingeniosa (clever) (line 4), fida (faithful) (line 6)**

Lines 7–8     What are the three imperatives in these lines? **accipe, perfer, pelle**

Line 10     What is the case and use of *tibi?* **dative of possession**

    What is the case and use of *ordine?* **ablative of comparison**

Line 11     What is the case and use of *te?* **accusative, subject of *sensisse* in indirect statement**

Line 12     What is the form of *tuere?* **imperative active singular (*tuor,* deponent)**

Line 13     What is the form of *agam?* **first person singular present subjunctive active**

    How is *agam* used? **indirect question**

    What is the subject of *vivere?* **me (understood)**

Line 14     What is the subject of *fert?* **cera**

Line 16     What is the form of *legat?* **third person singular present subjunctive active**

    How is *legat* used? **indirect command (after *fac*)**

Line 17     What is the form of *aspicias?* **second person singular present subjunctive active**

    How is *aspicias* used? **indirect command (after *mando*)**

Line 21     What is the subject of *moretur?* **littera (line 22)**

Line 27     What is the case and use of *Veneri?* **dative, indirect object of *dedicat* (line 28)**

## Multiple Choice Questions *Suggested time: 15 minutes*

1. The figure of speech employed in *neque ancillas inter habenda* (line 2) is
   - a. polysyndeton
   - b. ellipsis
   - c. hyperbaton
   - **d. hyperbole**

2. Another figure of speech in line 2, *ancillas inter,* is
   - a. metaphor
   - b. litotes
   - c. asyndeton
   - **d. prolepsis**

3. In line 3, *noctis* is called *furtivae* because
   - a. Nape is deceptive
   - **b. Ovid's relationship with Corinna is secretive/improper**
   - c. Ovid doesn't know when he will see Corinna
   - d. night is dark and secretive

4. Ovid tells us in line 9 that
   - a. Nape is cruel
   - b. Nape is hard-hearted
   - **c. Nape is soft-hearted**
   - d. Nape is not made of stone

5. In line 10, Ovid additionally describes Nape as one
   - a. who is too ambitious
   - **b. who is not overly sophisticated for her station**
   - c. who dresses with simplicity
   - d. who comes from the lower class

6. The metrical pattern for the first four feet of line 11 is
   - a. spondee-dactyl-spondee-dactyl
   - b. dactyl-spondee-dactyl-spondee
   - **c. dactyl-spondee-spondee-dactyl**
   - d. spondee-spondee-dactyl-dactyl

7. The figure of speech which Ovid uses in line 12 is
   - **a. metaphor**
   - b. personification
   - c. pleonasm
   - d. metonymy

8. In line 15, *vacuae* modifies
   - a. *tabellas*
   - b. *hora*
   - c. the speaker as indirect object
   - **d. *dominae* (understood)**

9. In lines 17–18, the poet asks
   - **a. Nape to watch Corinna while she reads the letter**
   - b. Corinna to be calm
   - c. to know the future
   - d. to read Corinna's face

10. In lines 19–24, the poet will settle for a reply
    - a. that comes right back
    - b. that doesn't tire Corinna
    - **c. that is a single word**
    - d. that will completely fill the tablet

11. The case of *vile* (line 28) is
    - a. ablative singular
    - b. nominative plural
    - c. accusative plural
    - **d. nominative singular**

12. The poet employs in line 28 the figure of speech known as
    - a. assonance
    - b. hyperbole
    - c. metaphor
    - **d. personification**

# Translation *Suggested time: 15 minutes*

Translate the passage below as literally as possible.

> si quaeret quid agam, spe noctis vivere dices;
>    cetera fert blanda cera notata manu.
> dum loquor, hora fugit: vacuae bene redde tabellas,
>    verum continuo fac tamen illa legat.
> 5  aspicias oculos mando frontemque legentis:
>    et tacito vultu scire futura licet.
> nec mora, perlectis rescribat multa iubeto:
>    odi, cum late splendida cera vacat.
>
> *Amores 1.11.13–20*

**If she will ask how I am doing, you will say that I live [but] by the hope of night-time; the wax marked with a caressing hand tells the rest. While I speak, time flies: deliver well [to your mistress] these tablets when she is unoccupied, but nevertheless see that she reads them immediately. I order you to look at her eyes and forehead while she is reading: it is also possible to know what will be from a silent countenance. And so that there be no delay, order that after she has read the tablets through she write back many things: I hate it when the shining wax is widely empty.**

**18 chunks. 9 points total, 1/2 point each. Round up to nearest whole point.**

| | |
|---|---|
| *si quaeret quid agam* | **if she will ask how I am doing** |
| *spe noctis vivere dices* | **you will say that I live [but] by the hope of nighttime** |
| *blanda cera notata manu* | **the wax, marked with a caressing hand** |
| *cetera fert* | **tells/bears the rest** |
| *dum loquor hora fugit* | **while I speak the hour flees** |
| *bene redde tabellas* | **deliver well the tablets** |
| *vacuae* | **to [your mistress] unoccupied** |
| *verum fac tamen* | **but nevertheless see/make that** |
| *continuo ... illa legat* | **she read them immediately/without delay** |
| *aspicias mando* | **I order you to look** |
| *oculos frontemque legentis* | **at her/the eyes and forehead while she is reading /of her while reading** |
| *et scire futura licet* | **it is also possible to know what will be** |
| *tacito vultu* | **from a silent countenance/expression** |
| *nec mora* | **and [that there be] no delay** |
| *rescribat multa iubeto* | **order that she write back many things/much** |
| *perlectis* | **after [the tablets] have been read/[the tablets] having been read** |
| *odi cum splendida cera* | **I hate when the shining wax** |
| *late vacat* | **is empty over a large area/broadly/widely** |

# Short Analysis Questions

1. In line 10, the poet refers to Nape's *simplicitas*. What characteristic of the maid is he describing here?

   **her lack of sophistication**

2. a. Write a literal translation of line 11 *credibile est et et te sensisse Cupidinis arcus*.

   **"It is likely that even you have felt Cupid's bow."**

   b. Why is this line a dubious compliment?

   **et te is concessive and suggests the improbability of one of Nape's station falling in love.**

3. To whom does the word *legentis* (line 17) refer?

   **Corinna (understood)**

4. What is the Latin word that must be understood in order to complete an ablative absolute with *perlectis* (line 19)?

   **tabellis (understood)**

5. In lines 25–28, the poet promises to reward the tablets if he gets a favorable reply from Corinna. Name two actions the poet will take and cite the Latin that expresses each.

   **(1) He will give the tablets a crown of victory (and place them in the middle of Venus's sanctuary).**

   **non ego victrices lauro redimire tabellas/nec Veneris media ponere in aede morer.**

   **(2) He will provide an inscription for the tablets.**

   **subscribam VENERI FIDAS SIBI NASO MINISTRAS/DEDICAT. AT NUPER VILE FUISTIS ACER.**

# Essay *Suggested time: 20 minutes*

In lines 19–24, Ovid describes the answer that he wishes to receive from Corinna. Write a short essay in which you discuss the contrast between the original reply that Ovid wants and the final reply that he requests. Consider the poet's reason for changing his request in your answer.

Support your assertions with appropriate references drawn from the poem. All Latin words must be copied or their line numbers provided, AND they must be translated or paraphrased closely enough so that it is clear you understand the Latin. It is your responsibility to convince your reader that you are basing your conclusions on the Latin text and not merely on a general recollection of the passage. Direct your answer to the question; do not merely summarize the passage. Please write your essay on a separate piece of paper.

**The question asks the student to perceive why the speaker's initial wish for a tablet filled by Corinna's response is changed to a request for a one-word answer. The change graphically underscores the speaker's anxiety and his need for a quick positive response to his letter. Students may point out lines**

that illustrate the speaker's original wish for a full tablet (lines 19–21), his growing anxiety (lines 8, 15, 19), and his rationalization that a full tablet may tire his lady (line 23) with which he tries to cover up his need for a simple, one-word "yes" reply. The grader should consider whether the student frames an argument that focuses on the way the poem illustrates the anxiety and uncertainty of the lover and looks at how well the Latin evidence is used in support of the analysis.

6 – A fully-developed essay that analyzes how Ovid shows the speaker's impatience and anxiety. The student uses ample and appropriate Latin passages in support of his argument. Only minor errors present.

5 – A strong essay, but one in which the argument is not fully developed. Latin references are properly cited. The student is familiar with the poem.

4 – A good essay, but one in which the student fails to consider fully the reasons for the speaker's change of request about Corinna's reply. Insufficient Latin examples are selected to support the arguments.

3 – A limited response where the Latin evidence is weak and/or inappropriate. The student describes the poem but does not analyze it. In some 3 papers, the student responds well to the question but does not use any Latin evidence.

2 – The student shows some understanding of the question, but the essay is vague and the Latin cited not well-chosen.

1 – The response lacks coherence. There is no substantial argument, and the student demonstrates no understanding of the poem.

0 – The response is irrelevant to the topic or incorrect, or merely restates the question without any analysis.

## Scansion

Scan the following lines.

credibil(e) est et te sensisse Cupidinis arcus:

in me militiae signa tuere tuae.

si quaeret quid agam, spe noctis vivere dices;

cetera fert blanda cera notata manu.

*Amores 1.11.11–14*

# Vocabulary

1. What two Latin words combine to form *colligo* (line 1)? Give each Latin word and its meaning.

   a. *cum*—with, along with

   b. *lego*—choose, select, pickout, read

2. Give the principal parts for the verb from which *dandis* (line 4) is formed. Give a meaning for each part.

   a. *do*—I give, do give, am giving

   b. *dedi*—I gave, did give, have given

   c. *dare*—to give

   d. *datus*—having been given

3. Give the principal parts for the verb from which *hortata* (line 5) is formed. Give a meaning for each part.

   a. *hortor*—I urge, do urge, am urging

   b. *hortari*—to urge

   c. *hortatus sum*—I urged, did urge, have urged

4. What two Latin words form *accipe* (line 7)? Give each Latin word and its meaning.

   a. *ad*—to or toward

   b. *capio*—I take, seize

5. Give the principal parts and meanings for *agam* (line 13).

   a. *ago*—I do

   b. *agere*—to do

   c. *egi*—I have done

   d. *actus*—having been done

6. Give the principal parts and meanings for *loquor* (line 15).

   a. *loquor*—I speak, do speak, am speaking

   b. *loqui*—to speak

   c. *locutus sum*—I spoke, did speak, have spoken

7.  *fac* (line 16) is an irregular imperative. List the other monosyllabic imperatives in Latin and give their meanings.

    a.  *dic*—speak, tell

    b.  *duc*—lead

    c.  *fer*—carry

    d.  *i*—go

8.  a.  What kind of a verb is *licet* (line 18)?  **an impersonal verb**

    b.  Translate *licet.*  **it is allowed**

9.  Give the principal parts and meanings for the verb from which *perlectis* (line 19) is formed.

    a.  *perlego*—I read through

    b.  *perlegere*— to read through

    c.  *perlegi*—I have read through

    d.  *perlectus*—having been read through

10. Give the two Latin words and their meanings that combine to create this verb.

    a.  *per*—through

    b.  *lego*—read

11. Give the principal parts and meanings for *morer* (line 26).

    a.  *moror*— delay

    b.  *morari*—to delay

    c.  *moratus sum*—I have delayed

# AMORES 1.12

Flete meos casus: tristes rediere tabellae;
    infelix hodie littera posse negat.
omina sunt aliquid: modo cum discedere vellet,
    ad limen digitos restitit icta Nape.
5     missa foras iterum limen transire memento
    cautius atque alte sobria ferre pedem.
ite hinc, difficiles, funebria ligna, tabellae,
    tuque, negaturis cera referta notis,
quam, puto, de longae collectam flore cicutae
10    melle sub infami Corsica misit apis.
at tamquam minio penitus medicata rubebas:
    ille color vere sanguinulentus erat.
proiectae triviis iaceatis, inutile lignum,
    vosque rotae frangat praetereuntis onus.
15   illum etiam, qui vos ex arbore vertit in usum,
    convincam puras non habuisse manus.
praebuit illa arbor misero suspendia collo,
    carnifici diras praebuit illa cruces;
illa dedit turpes raucis bubonibus umbras,
20    vulturis in ramis et strigis ova tulit.
his ego commisi nostros insanus amores
    molliaque ad dominam verba ferenda dedi?
aptius hae capiant vadimonia garrula cerae,
    quas aliquis duro cognitor ore legat;
25   inter ephemeridas melius tabulasque iacerent,
    in quibus absumptas fleret avarus opes.
ergo ego vos rebus duplices pro nomine sensi:
    auspicii numerus non erat ipse boni.
quid precer iratus, nisi vos cariosa senectus
30    rodat, et immundo cera sit alba situ?

## Short Answer Questions

Line 1      What is the form of *rediere*? **alternative third person plural perfect indicative active (*redierunt*)**

              What is its subject? ***tristes tabellae***

Line 2      The subject for the infinitive *posse* is missing. What is the subject? ***eam* or *dominam* or *Corinnam***

              What complementary infinitive for *posse* is missing? ***venire***

| Line 3 | What is the form of *vellet*? **third person singular imperfect subjunctive active** |
|---|---|
| | How is this form used? ***cum* circumstantial** |
| Line 4 | What is the case and use of *digitos*? **accusative of body part affected, a Greek accusative** |
| Line 8 | What is the case and use of the two words *negaturis . . . notis*? **ablative of means** |
| | What is the form of *negaturis*? **future active participle** |
| | Translate the two words *negaturis . . . notis*. **"notes that will (are about to) say no"** |
| Line 11 | What is the form of *medicata*? **perfect passive participle (of *medico*)** |
| | What does it modify? ***cera* (line 8)** |
| Line 13 | What is the form of *iaceatis*? **second person plural present subjunctive active** |
| | How is this form used? **jussive/hortatory** |
| | Translate *iaceatis*. **"may you lie"** |
| Line 14 | What is the form of *praetereuntis*? **present active participle** |
| | Of which irregular verb is this a compound? ***eo, ire, i(vi)*** |
| Line 15 | What is the case and use of *illum*? **accusative, subject of infinitive *habuisse* (line 16)** |
| Line 18 | What is the case and use of *carnifici*? **dative, indirect object of *praebuit*** |
| Line 22 | What is the form of *ferenda*? **future passive participle** |
| | Translate *ferenda*. **"(about) to be carried, that must be carried"** |
| Line 24 | What is the antecedent for *quas*? ***cerae* (line 23)** |
| | What is the form of *legat*? **third person singular present subjunctive active** |
| | How is this form used? **subjunctive by attraction to potential subjunctive, *capiant* (line 23)** |
| Line 28 | What is the case and use of the two words *auspicii . . . boni*? **genitive of quality/description** |
| Line 29 | What is the form of *precer*? **first person singular present subjunctive active (deponent)** |
| | How is this form used? **deliberative subjunctive** |

# Multiple Choice Questions *Suggested time: 13 minutes*

1. Whom does the poet address in *flete* (line 1)?
   a. Corinna
   b. Nape
   **c. his audience/readers**
   d. Corinna and Nape together

2. Why does the poet call the tablets *funebria ligna* (line 7)?
   a. the wood is poisonous
   **b. the wood is unlucky**
   c. the poet wants to die
   d. Corinna has died

3. What is the figure of speech used in lines 7 and 11?
   a. hyperbole
   b. metonymy
   c. pleonasm
   **d. personification**

4. Why does the poet call the wood *inutile* (line 13)?
   **a. the tablets have failed to carry back a favorable message**
   b. the wood of the tablets cannot be used again
   c. the wood of the tablets has been broken
   d. the wood of the tablets has been thrown away

5. In line 19, the word order is a poetic figure of speech called
   a. golden line
   b. interlocked
   **c. chiasmus**
   d. ellipsis

6. The poet is *insanus* in line 21 because
   a. he committed his words to the tablets
   **b. he entrusted his love to the tablets**
   c. Corinna does not love him
   d. his message was too gentle

7. The metrical pattern for the first four feet of line 23 is
   **a. dactyl-dactyl-dactyl-dactyl**
   b. dactyl-spondee-dactyl-dactyl
   c. spondee-dactyl-spondee-dactyl
   d. dactyl-dactyl-dactyl-spondee

8. From lines 27–28, we learn that the poet calls the tablets *duplices* because
   a. they are truthful
   b. they are cruel
   c. they are made of wax
   **d. they have two halves**

9. The poet is *iratus* in line 29 because
   a. the tablets were unlucky
   **b. he cannot visit Corinna tonight**
   c. the tablets are eroding
   d. the wax has turned white

10. In line 29, *nisi* is best translated as
    a. unless
    **b. if not that**
    c. so that
    d. except that

11. The adjective *alba* (line 30) contrasts to the wax's original color which was
    a. blue
    c. black
    **b. red**
    d. yellow

## Translation *Suggested time: 10 minutes*

Translate the passage below as literally as possible.

> his ego commisi nostros insanus amores
>     molliaque ad dominam verba ferenda dedi?
> aptius hae capiant vadimonia garrula cerae,
>     quas aliquis duro cognitor ore legat;
> 5    inter ephemeridas melius tabulasque iacerent,
>     in quibus absumptas fleret avarus opes.

*Amores 1.12.21–26*

**Did I, insane, entrust my love to these and did I give gentle words [to these] to be carried to my mistress? These waxes, which some attorney might read with an uncaring mouth, may more suitably capture wordy promises at court appearances; they would lie better among diaries and account books in which the miser might weep over his spent wealth.**

**18 chunks. 9 points total, 1/2 point each. Round up to nearest whole point.**

| | |
|---|---|
| *insanus* | **insane/insanely** |
| *his ego commisi* | **did I entrust to these** |
| *nostros amores* | **my love** |
| *molliaque verba* | **and my gentle/soft/smooth words** |
| *ferenda* | **to be carried** |
| *ad dominam* | **to my mistress** |
| *dedi* | **did I give** |
| *aptius hae capiant . . . cerae* | **these waxes may/would more aptly capture** |
| *vadimonia garrula* | **wordy promises at court appearances/wordy securities [to appear in court]** |
| *quas aliquis cognitor* | **that some attorney** |
| *legat* | **may read** |
| *duro ore* | **with an uncaring/unsympathetic mouth** |
| *melius iacerent* | **they would better lie** |
| *inter ephemeridas* | **among diaries** |
| *tabulasque* | **and account books** |
| *in quibus* | **in which** |
| *fleret avarus* | **the/a miser might weep over** |
| *absumptas opes* | **his spent wealth** |

# Short Analysis Questions

1.  a.  Translate lines 3–6.

    > omina sunt aliquid: modo cum discedere vellet,
    >      ad limen digitos restitit icta Nape.
    > missa foras iterum limen transire memento
    >      cautius atque alte sobria ferre pedem.

    **"Omens are worth something: just now when she desired to leave, Nape struck her toe and lingered at the threshold. Remember the next time you are sent out of doors to cross the threshold more carefully and, sober, lift your foot high."**

    b.  Explain exactly to what real omen the poet refers in these lines.

    **For the Romans, striking one's foot when entering or leaving a room is a sign of bad luck.**

2.  In lines 7–10, the poet curses the tablets and the wax.

    a.  Give two Latin examples of how the wax is cursed. Translate your examples.

    **de longae collectam flore cicutae—"collected from the flower of the tall hemlock"**

    **melle sub infami Corsica misit apis—"the Corsican bee sent underneath the infamous honey"**

    b.  Explain *melle sub infami* (line 10). How can the wax be sent under the honey?

    **The wax is put in the bottom of the jar containing the honey.**

3.  In line 13, the poet suggests that the tablets be cast out at the crossroads, the meeting of three ways. To what might this be a reference?

    **The reference is to King Oedipus of Thebes, who met and killed his father at the crossroads, the place where three roads met.**

4.  In lines 15–20, the poet gives four reasons why the wood is unlucky. State two of the reasons, giving the Latin and translating it:

    a.  **puras non habuisse manus—the woodcutter's hands were impure**

    b.  **misero suspendia collo—the tree was used to hang people by the wretched neck**
        **OR**
        **diras praebuit cruces—the tree provided wood for crucifixions**
        **OR**
        **raucis bubonibus umbras/vulturis ... strigis ova— the tree offered roosts for horned and screech owls and for vultures**

5.  What are the best uses of the tablets according to lines 23–26? Use Latin words in your response.

    a.  **to capture wordy promises at court appearances—capiant vadimonia garrula**

    b.  **for use for diaries and account books on which the miser records and mourns his lost wealth—ephemeridas tabulas ... in quibus absumptas fleret avarus opes.**

6. How do the uses described in lines 23–26 contrast to those for which the poet employed the tablets?

> **These uses come from the world of *negotium*, law and business. Ovid had tried to use the tablets for pursuing *otium*—the leisure required for lovemaking.**

## Essay *Suggested time: 20 minutes*

*Amores* 1.11 and 1.12 are a pair, written to be read as a unit. Write an essay in which you compare the personification of the tablets in both poems. Pay particular attention to the poet's promise in 1.11.27–28 and his prayer in 1.12.29–30. How do these contrasting personifications affect the two poems?

Support your assertions with references drawn from **throughout** both poems. All Latin words must be copied or their line numbers provided, AND they must be translated or paraphrased closely enough so that it is clear you understand the Latin. It is your responsibility to convince your reader that you are basing your conclusions on the Latin text and not merely on a general recollection of the passage. Direct your answer to the question; do not merely summarize the passage. Please write your essay on a separate piece of paper.

**This question asks the student to consider how and why the writing tablets are personified in *Amores* 1.11 and 1.12. The student is directed to specific passages where the personification occurs and to consider why the tablets are personified and how the personifications differ before and after the speaker has received his reply. The student should point out that in 1.11 the speaker views the tablets as assistants for his potential victory and promises to crown them with laurels, while in 1.12, the speaker has learned that he cannot visit his lady and curses them for their deceitfulness and wishes that they age in neglect. The grader should look at the student's analysis of the personification in each of the two poems and at the argument that the student presents to explain the changes in personification. The grader should consider whether the student describes, rather than analyzes, the personifications and how well the Latin examples are cited and explained.**

**6 – A fully-developed essay that considers the two personifications as complementary and analyzes their function in the two poems. The student presents a fully supported argument. Ample references to the Latin text are given and they are properly cited. There may be a few minor errors.**

**5 – A strong essay, but with an argument that is not fully developed. Latin references are properly cited, and the essay demonstrates familiarity with both poems.**

**4 – A good response, but one that is uneven in its treatment, giving for example, a full explanation of one personification only. The discussion may be more descriptive than analytical, and the Latin support may be insufficient.**

**3 – A limited response where the Latin support is insufficient and/or irrelevant. Or, the student presents a fairly reasoned argument but uses no Latin to support it.**

**2 – The essay shows some understanding of the question, but is far too general. The Latin is inadequately or incorrectly cited.**

**1** – The essay has no coherence, no real argument, and no real understanding of the two poems.

**0** – The response is irrelevant to the topic or incorrect, or merely restates the question without any analysis.

# Scansion

Scan the following lines.

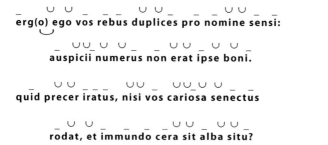

*Amores 1.12.27–30*

# Vocabulary

List the nouns, adjectives, and verbs with negative connotations in this poem. Provide the dictionary entry for the words you list. List the participles as adjectives. Provide line references in parentheses beside your Latin choices.

**Nouns**

1. *casus, -us* (m.) misfortune (line 1)

2. *omen, ominis* (n.) omen (line 3)

3. *cicuta, -ae* (f.) hemlock (line 9)

4. *trivium, -ii.* (n.) crossroad (line 13)

5. *suspendium, -ii.* (n.) hanging (line 17)

6. *carnifex, -icis* (m.) executioner (line 18)

7. *crux, cruces* (f.) cross (line 18)

8. *bubo, bubonis* (m.) horned owl (line 19)

9. *umbra, -ae* (f.) darkness (line 19)

10. *vultur, -is* (m.) vulture (line 20)

11. *strix, strigis* (m.) screech owl (line 20)

12. *avarus, -i* (m.) miser (line 26)

13. *senectus, -us* (m.) old age (line 29)

14. *situs, -us* (m.) neglect (line 30)

## Adjectives

1. *tristis, -e* dismal (line 1)

2. *infelix, -icis* unfortunate, unlucky (line 2)

3. *ictus, -a, -um* struck, having been beaten (line 4)

4. *sobrius, -a, -um* sober (line 6)

5. *difficilis, -e* difficult (line 7)

6. *funebris, -e* deadly, funereal (line 7)

7. *negaturus, -a, -um* about to say no, who will say no (line 8)

8. *infamis, -e* infamous, disgraced (line 10)

9. *sanguinulentus, -a, -um* blood-red (line 12)

10. *inutilis, -e* useless (line 13)

11. *miser, -a, -um* wretched (line 17)

12. *dirus, -a, -um* dreadful, awful (line 18)

13. *turpis, -e* loathsome, repulsive (line19)

14. *raucus, -a, -um* harsh sounding (line 19)

15. *insanus, -a, -um* frenzied, mad (line 21)

16. *durus, -a, -um* stubborn, hard (line 24)

17. *absumptus, -a, -um* squandered, used up (line 26)

18. *duplex, -icis* deceitful (line 27)

19. *iratus, -a, -um* angry, furious (line 29)

20. *cariosus, -a, -um* decayed, withered (line 29)

21. *immundus, -a, -um* unclean, foul (line 30)

## Verbs

1. *fleo, flere, flevi, fletum* weep (lines 1 & 26)

2. *nego, negare, negavi, negatum* to say no, deny (line 2)

3. *frango, frangere, fregi, fractum* to break (line 14)

4. *rodo, rodere, rosi, rosum* to eat away, erode (line 30)

# AMORES 3.15

Quaere novum vatem, tenerorum mater Amorum:
    raditur haec elegis ultima meta meis;
quos ego composui, Paeligni ruris alumnus,
    (nec me deliciae dedecuere meae)
5  si quid id est, usque a proavis vetus ordinis heres,
    non modo militiae turbine factus eques.
Mantua Vergilio gaudet, Verona Catullo;
    Paelignae dicar gloria gentis ego,
quam sua libertas ad honesta coegerat arma,
10    cum timuit socias anxia Roma manus.
atque aliquis spectans hospes Sulmonis aquosi
    moenia, quae campi iugera pauca tenent,
"quae tantum" dicet "potuistis ferre poetam,
    quantulacumque estis, vos ego magna voco."
15  culte puer puerique parens Amathusia culti,
    aurea de campo vellite signa meo:
corniger increpuit thyrso graviore Lyaeus;
    pulsanda est magnis area maior equis.
imbelles elegi, genialis Musa, valete,
20    post mea mansurum fata superstes opus.

## Short Answer Questions

| | | |
|---|---|---|
| Line 1 | What is the form of *quaere*? | **singular present imperative active** |
| Line 2 | What is the case and use of the two words *elegis . . . meis*? | **ablative of means** |
| Line 3 | What is the case and use of *quos*? | **accusative, direct object of *composui*** |
| Line 4 | What is the form of *dedecuere*? | **third person plural perfect indicative active (alternate form of *dedecuerunt*)** |
| | What is the case and use of the two words *deliciae . . . meae*? | **nominative, subject of *dedecuere*** |
| Line 7 | What is the case and use of *Vergilio* and *Catullo*? | **ablative with *gaudet*/ablative of cause** |
| Line 9 | What is the antecedent for *quam*? | ***Paelignae gentis* (line 8)** |
| | What is the case and use of *quam*? | **accusative, direct object of *coegerat*** |
| Line 12 | What is the case and use of *campi*? | **partitive genitive/genitive of the whole** |

| Line 13 | What is the antecedent for *quae*? **moenia (line 12)** |
| Line 13 | What is the case and use of *quae*? **nominative, subject of *potuistis*** |
| Line 16 | What is the form of *vellite*? **plural present imperative active** |
| Line 17 | What is the case and use of *thyrso graviore*? **ablative of means** |
| Line 18 | What is the form of *pulsanda*? **future passive participle (gerundive)** |
| Line 20 | What is the form of *mansurum*? **future active participle** |

## Multiple Choice Questions *Suggested time: 12 minutes*

1.  Whom does the poet address in *quaere* (line 1)?
    - a. his mother
    - **b. Venus**
    - c. Corinna
    - d. Cupid

2.  Line 2 (*raditur . . . meis*) is best translated as
    - **a. this final goal post is grazed by my elegies**
    - b. I have grazed the final goal post with my elegies
    - c. my elegies have grazed the final goal post
    - d. these are my final elegies at the goal post

3.  The case of *deliciae* in line 4 is
    - **a. nominative**
    - b. genitive
    - c. dative
    - d. vocative

4.  The metrical pattern of the first four feet of line 13 is
    - a. dactyl-spondee-dactyl-spondee
    - b. spondee-dactyl-dactyl-spondee
    - **c. spondee-spondee-dactyl-spondee**
    - d. spondee-dactyl-spondee-dactyl

5.  In line 15, the words *culte* and *culti* represent what figure of speech?
    - a. hyperbaton
    - **b. polyptoton**
    - c. hendiadys
    - d. hysteron proteron

6.  In line 16, *vellite* is directed towards
    - a. Apollo
    - b. Cupid
    - c. Venus and Apollo
    - **d. Cupid and Venus**

7.  In line 16, *campo meo* is an ablative of
    - a. manner
    - **b. separation**
    - c. instrument
    - d. comparison

8. To what god does *corniger Lyaeus* (line 17) refer?

    a. Mars                                  b. Venus

    c. Cupid                                **d. Bacchus**

9. When the poet refers to *magnis area maior equis* (line 18) he means

    a. that he is going to drive a team of horses     b. that his poetry will be concerned with greater love

    c. that he will travel to great lands     **d. that he will undertake a new and grander kind of poetry**

10. Line 20 (*post . . . opus*) is best translated:

    a. [farewell] my work which will remain after my fates     **b. [farewell] my surviving work which will remain after my death**

    c. [farewell] after my death you will remain my work     d. [farewell] you who will not remain fated after my work

## Translation *Suggested time: 15 minutes*

Translate the passage below as literally as possible.

> Mantua Vergilio gaudet, Verona Catullo;
>    Paelignae dicar gloria gentis ego,
> quam sua libertas ad honesta coegerat arma,
>    cum timuit socias anxia Roma manus.
> 5   atque aliquis spectans hospes Sulmonis aquosi
>    moenia, quae campi iugera pauca tenent,
> "quae tantum" dicet "potuistis ferre poetam,
>    quantulacumque estis, vos ego magna voco."

*Amores 3.15.7–14*

**Mantua rejoices in its Vergil, Verona in its Catullus; I shall be called the glory of the Paelignian race, whom its own liberty had forced to [bear] honorable arms, when troubled Rome feared their fellow forces. And some visitor looking upon the walls of watery Sulmo, which encompass but a few acres of field, will say "You who have been able to bear so great a poet, however small you are, I shall call you great."**

**18 chunks. 9 points total, 1/2 point each. Round up to nearest whole point.**

| | |
|---|---|
| *Mantua Vergilio gaudet* | **Mantua rejoices in Vergil** |
| *Verona Catullo* | **Verona in Catullus** |
| *dicar ego* | **I shall be called** |
| *Paelignae . . . gloriae gentis* | **the glory of the Palignian race** |
| *quam sua libertas* | **whom its own liberty** |
| *ad honesta coegerat arma* | **had forced into honorable arms** |

| | |
|---|---|
| cum timuit anxia Roma | when troubled Rome feared |
| socias manus | their fellow/allied armed forces |
| atque aliquis hospes | and some visitor/guest |
| spectans moenia | looking upon the walls |
| Sulmonis aquosi | of watery Sulmo |
| quae tenent | which encompass/hold |
| campi iugera pauca | a few acres of field |
| dicet | will say |
| quae potuistis ferre | you who were/have been able to bear |
| tantum poetam | so great a poet |
| quantulacumque estis | however small you are |
| vos ego magna voco | You I call great |

## Short Analysis Questions

1. What are the two meanings for *deliciae* in line 4?

   a. **beloved**

   b. **the poems**

2. In line 6, the poet refers to the *militiae turbine*. What does this phrase mean literally and why does Ovid view it as inappropriate for himself?

   ***militiae turbine* means "by the whirlwind of military service." Ovid indicates that he is an *eques* by birth and not by recent military appointment.**

3. To what historical event does line 10 *cum timuit socias anxia Roma manus* refer?

   **The Social War 91–87 BCE**

4. Translate *aurea de campo vellite signa meo* (line 16).

   **"Withdraw your golden standards from my camp."**

5. Who is the *genialis Musa* referred to in line 19?

   **Ovid's personal creative muse or Erato, muse of elegiac poetry**

# Essay *Suggested time: 20 minutes*

This poem, the last of the *Amores*, contains the poet's farewell to elegiac poetry and articulates his intention to write tragic poetry. The poem contains, as well, the poet's assessment of what he has accomplished. Write a short essay in which you summarize Ovid's self-evaluation of his and his poetry's worth.

Support your assertions with references drawn from **throughout** the poem. All Latin words must be copied or their line numbers provided, AND they must be translated or paraphrased closely enough so that it is clear you understand the Latin. It is your responsibility to convince your reader that you are basing your conclusions on the Latin text and not merely on a general recollection of the passage. Direct your answer to the question; do not merely summarize the passage. Please write your essay on a separate piece of paper.

**Although this essay question uses the word "summarize," the student is being asked to analyze the speaker's self-evaluation in the context of the individual poem and the collection. The grader should look for an essay that presents an argument that defends a clear statement about the speaker's view of his work in the poem, an essay that demonstrates that although the speaker expresses the intention to give up elegiac poetry, he places himself among the great poets (lines 7–10) and believes that his work will be remembered long after his death (line 20). The student should consider the purpose of the farewell and the seriousness of the intention to give up elegy for tragedy (lines 15–18) in the context of the self-praise that the poem offers.**

**The essay should not simply list the points the speaker makes. In addition, it should use Latin examples effectively, both citing them and commenting on their significance.**

**6 – A clearly focused essay that makes a strong argument and supports it amply with Latin examples. The student perceives the possible double meanings of the poet's statement of farewell. There are only a few very minor errors of translation or interpretation.**

**5 – A strong essay that provides a good central argument but may not be fully supported with sufficient references to the poem. The Latin examples are correctly cited.**

**4 – A satisfactory response, but one that does not develop its arguments sufficiently. The discussion may be merely a summary. Latin support is not extensive.**

**3 – A limited essay in that the Latin is inappropriate and not correctly cited, and there is little or no analysis.**

**2 – There is some understanding of the passage, but the essay is far too general. The student shows little comprehension of the cited Latin.**

**1 – The response is incoherent. There may be some pertinent information, but it is not connected to any clear argument.**

**0 – The response is irrelevant to the topic or incorrect, or merely restates the question without any analysis.**

# Scansion

Scan the following lines.

```
  _  U  U _    _  _    U U _  _    _ U U _  _
Quaere novum vatem, tenerorum mater Amorum:
```

```
   _ UU  _  UU _ U  U _U  U_
raditur haec elegis ultima meta meis;
```

```
  _ U U  _   UU_   _  _   _ U U _   _
quos ego composui, Paeligni ruris alumnus,
```

```
   _   _ _UU_   _ UU_U  U_
(nec me deliciae dedecuere meae)
```

Amores 3.15.1–4

# Vocabulary

1. List the six nouns in the poem that identify the poet. Provide the dictionary entry and principal meaning for the words you list. Provide line references in parentheses beside each Latin noun.

   a. *vates, -is* (m.) poet (line 1)

   b. *alumnus, -i* (m.) a "son" or "foster son" (line 3)

   c. *heres, -is* (m.) heir (line 5)

   d. *eques, -is* (m.) member of the equestrian order (line 6)

   e. *gloria, -ae* (f.) glory (line 8)

   f. *poeta, -ae* (m.) poet (line 13)

2. List the six adjectives relating to physical or metaphorical size or weight in the poem. Provide the dictionary entry and principal meaning for the words you list. Provide line references in parentheses beside each Latin adjective.

   a. *pauci, -ae, -a* few (line 12)

   b. *tantus, -a, -um* so great (line 13)

   c. *quantuluscumque, -acumque, -umcumque* however small (line 14)

   d. *magnus, -a, -um* great (line 14)

   e. *gravior, graviore* heavier (line 17)

   f. *magnus, -a, -um* great (line 18)

3. List the four participles in the poem. Give an exact translation for each participle and provide the principal parts of the verb from which each comes. Provide line references in parentheses beside each Latin participle.

   a. *factus*—having been made—*facio, facere, feci, factum* (line 6)

   b. *spectans*—looking at—*specto, -are, -avi, -atum* (line 11)

   c. *pulsanda*—must be beaten—*pulso, -are, -avi, -atum* (line 18)

   d. *mansurum*—about to remain—*maneo, -ere, mansi, mansurum* (line 20)

4. List the five verbs in the perfect or pluperfect tense in the poem. Translate the form and give the principal parts for its verb. Provide line references in parentheses beside each Latin verb.

   a. *composui*—I composed, did compose, have composed—*compono, -ere, composui, compositum* (line 3)

   b. *dedecuere*—they dishonored, did dishonor, have dishonored—*dedecet, -ere, -uit* (line 4)

   c. *coegerat*—he had forced/compelled—*cogo, -ere, coegi, coactus* (line 9)

   d. *potuistis*—you could—*possum, posse, potui* (line 13)

   e. *increpuit*—he rattled, did rattle, has rattled—*increpo, -are, -ui, -itum* (line 17)

5. Provide the dictionary entry and English meaning for each of the following.

   a. *meta* **meta, -ae (f.) turning post**

   b. *proavis* **proavus, -i (m.) forefather**

   c. *ordinis* **ordo, -inis (m.) class, rank**

   d. *heres* **heres, -edis (m.) heir**

   e. *eques* **eques, -quitis (m.) member of the equestrian order**

   f. *hospes* **hospes, -itis (m.) visitor**

   g. *iugera* **iugerum, -i (n.) two thirds of an acre**

   h. *thyrso* **thyrsus, -i (m.) wand**

# TEXT SELECTIONS FROM THE *METAMORPHOSES* WITH EXERCISES & ANSWERS

# APOLLO AND DAPHNE
# METAMORPHOSES 1.452–487

Primus amor Phoebi Daphne Peneia, quem non
fors ignara dedit, sed saeva Cupidinis ira,
Delius hunc nuper, victa serpente superbus,
455    viderat adducto flectentem cornua nervo
"quid" que "tibi, lascive puer, cum fortibus armis?"
dixerat: "ista decent umeros gestamina nostros,
qui dare certa ferae, dare vulnera possumus hosti,
qui modo pestifero tot iugera ventre prementem
460    stravimus innumeris tumidum Pythona sagittis.
tu face nescio quos esto contentus amores
*provoke* — inritare tua, nec laudes adsere nostras!"    *to lay claim to*
filius huic Veneris "figat tuus omnia, Phoebe,
te meus arcus" ait; "quantoque animalia cedunt
465    cuncta deo, tanto minor est tua gloria nostra."
dixit et eliso percussis aere pennis
inpiger umbrosa Parnasi constitit arce
eque sagittifera prompsit duo tela pharetra
diversorum operum: fugat hoc, facit illud amorem;
470    quod facit, auratum est et cuspide fulget acuta,
quod fugat, obtusum est et habet sub harundine plumbum.
hoc deus in nympha Peneide fixit, at illo
laesit Apollineas traiecta per ossa medullas;
protinus alter amat, fugit altera nomen amantis
475    silvarum latebris captivarumque ferarum
exuviis gaudens innuptaeque aemula Phoebes:
vitta coercebat positos sine lege capillos.
multi illam petiere, illa aversata petentes
inpatiens expersque viri nemora avia lustrat
480    nec, quid Hymen, quid Amor, quid sint conubia curat.
saepe pater dixit: "generum mihi, filia, debes,"
saepe pater dixit: "debes mihi, nata, nepotes";
illa velut crimen taedas exosa iugales
pulchra verecundo suffuderat ora rubore
485    inque patris blandis haerens cervice lacertis
"da mihi perpetua, genitor carissime," dixit
"virginitate frui! dedit hoc pater ante Dianae."

# Short Answer Questions

| | | |
|---|---|---|
| Line 454 | What grammatical construction does *victa serpente* form? | **ablative absolute** |
| Line 458 | What is the case and use of *hosti*? | **dative, indirect object of *dare*** |
| Line 462 | What word does *tua* modify? | **face (line 461)** |
| Line 464 | Of which verb is *te* the accusative direct object? | **figat (line 463)** |
| Line 468 | What is the case and use of *duo*? | **accusative plural modifying *tela*** |
| | What is the case and use of *pharetra*? | **ablative, object of *eque (ex et)*** |
| Line 474 | To whom does *alter* refer? | **Apollo** |
| | To whom does *altera* refer? | **Daphne** |
| Line 478 | What is the person, number, and tense of *petiere*? | **third person plural perfect** |
| | To whom does *illa* refer? | **Daphne** |
| Line 484 | What is the case and use of *ora*? | **accusative, direct object of *suffuderat*** |

# Multiple Choice Questions *Suggested time: 12 minutes*

1. In lines 452–453, we learn that
   a. **Cupid is responsible for Apollo's love for Daphne**
   b. Daphne's father, Peneus, is responsible for the love between Apollo and Daphne
   c. Apollo fell in love with Daphne by chance
   d. Apollo was the first ever to love Daphne

2. In line 455, *flectentem* refers to
   a. Daphne
   b. Apollo
   c. Delius
   d. **Cupid**

3. The metrical pattern for the first four feet of line 456 is
   a. **dactyl-spondee-dactyl-spondee**
   b. dactyl-dactyl-spondee-dactyl
   c. spondee-spondee-dactyl-dactyl
   d. dactyl-spondee-dactyl-dactyl

4. In line 459, *prementem* describes
   a. *qui* (line 459)
   b. *iugera* (line 459)
   c. *tumidum* (line 460)
   d. **Pythona (line 460)**

5. Which of the following figures of speech can be found in lines 461–462 (*tu face . . . inritare tua*)?
   a. hysteron proteron
   **b. hyperbaton**
   c. hendiadys
   d. hyperbole

6. The best translation for the two words *nec . . . adsere* (line 462) is
   a. not to lay claim to
   b. they did not lay claim to
   c. they have not laid claim to
   **d. do not lay claim to**

7. The intent of Cupid's speech to Apollo in lines 463–465 (*figat . . . nostra*) is
   **a. to boast to Apollo**
   b. to glorify Apollo
   c. to advise Apollo
   d. to confuse Apollo

8. The antecedent of *quod* (line 470) is
   a. *operum* (line 469)
   b. *pharetra* (line 468)
   **c. *illud* (line 469)**
   d. *amorem* (line 469)

9. In line 476, *gaudens* refers to
   **a. Daphne**
   b. Apollo
   c. hiding places
   d. animal skins

10. In line 478, *aversata* is best translated
    a. rejecting
    b. having been rejected
    **c. having rejected**
    d. being rejected

## Translation *Suggested time: 10 minutes*

Translate the passage below as literally as possible.

> hoc deus in nympha Peneide fixit, at illo
> laesit Apollineas traiecta per ossa medullas;
> protinus alter amat, fugit altera nomen amantis
> silvarum latebris captivarumque ferarum
> 5    exuviis gaudens innuptaeque aemula Phoebes:
> vitta coercebat positos sine lege capillos.

*Metamorphoses 1.472–477*

**This one the god lodged in Peneus's maiden daughter, but with that other one he injured Apollo's marrow through his pierced bones. Immediately one falls in love; the other flees the name of lover, rejoicing in the hiding places of the forests and in the spoils of hunted animals and as a female companion of Diana. A headband bound up her hair arranged without order.**

**18 chunks. 9 points total, 1/2 point each. Round up to nearest whole point.**

| | |
|---|---|
| hoc deus ... fixit | this one the god fixed/lodged |
| in nympha Peneide | in the Peneian nymph/in Peneus's maiden daughter |
| at illo | but with that other one |
| laesit | he injured/harmed |
| Apollineas ... medullas | Apollo's marrow/the Apollonian marrow |
| traiecta per ossa | through his pierced bones |
| protinus alter amat | immediately one falls in love |
| fugit altera | the other flees |
| nomen amantis | the name of lover |
| gaudens | rejoicing |
| silvarum latebris | in the hiding places of the forests |
| exuviis ... -que | and in the spoils |
| captivarum-... ferarum | of captured/hunted wild animals |
| aemula ... -que | and as a female companion/imitator |
| innuptae-... Phoebes | of unmarried Diana |
| vitta coercebat | a headband/fillet bound up |
| positos ... capillos | her hair arranged |
| sine lege | without order/care |

# Short Analysis Questions

1. Without translating, briefly state what we learn about Apollo in these words: *victa serpente superbus* (line 454).

   **He is proud/haughty because of the heroic deed he accomplished; his recent defeat, with innumerable arrows, of the Python that had been plaguing the surrounding countryside.**

2. Identify a synthesis in line 458. Write out the Latin that expresses it and explain why it qualifies as a synthesis.

   **Line 458 contains three possible overlapping sets of syntheses:**

   **A   B   A   B**
   ***dare, certa, dare, vulnera***

   **A   B   A   B**
   ***dare, ferae, dare, hosti***

   **A   B   A   B**
   ***certa, ferae, vulnera, hosti***

   **This line with its overlapping interlocked word patterns highlights Apollo's great skill as an archer and by extension Ovid's great skill as a poet.**

3. Explain the action that happens in lines 466–469.

   **In these lines Cupid flies to the top of Mt. Parnassus, sacred to the Muses, where he chooses his two arrows of opposite purposes from his quiver. One is of gold and inspires love; the other has lead at its base and causes its victim to despise love.**

# Vocabulary

Below you will find a list of high frequency words you have encountered in your recent readings. For all the words you know, write out full dictionary entries, including English meanings, and put a √ mark in the left-hand column to show you have already committed these words to memory. For any words you do not yet know, write out the dictionary entries using the end glossary and learn them as soon as possible.

√

1. _____ alter _____

2. _____ ambō _____

3. _____ atque _____

4. _____ campus _____

5. _____ capillus _____

6. _____ cēdō _____

7. _____ cornū _____

8. _____ crīmen _____

9. _____ domina _____

10. _____ dūrus _____

11. _____ ferus _____

12. _____ fīgō _____

13. _____ gaudeō _____

14. _____ legō _____

15. _____ mittō _____

16. _____ modo _____

17. _____ multus _____

18. _____ negō _____

19. _____ nōmen _____

20. _____ nōn _____

21. _____ nūper _____

22. ____ *ōs* _____

23. ____ *petō* _____

24. ____ *pharetra* _____

25. ____ *possum* _____

26. ____ *premō* _____

27. ____ *prīmus* _____

28. ____ *puer* _____

29. ____ *saepe* _____

30. ____ *silva* _____

31. ____ *sine* _____

32. ____ *tuus* _____

33. ____ *vincō* _____

# APOLLO AND DAPHNE
# METAMORPHOSES 1.488–524

     ille quidem obsequitur, sed te decor iste quod optas
     esse vetat, votoque tuo tua forma repugnat:
490   Phoebus amat visaeque cupit conubia Daphnes,
     quodque cupit, sperat, suaque illum oracula fallunt,
     utque leves stipulae demptis adolentur aristis,
     ut facibus saepes ardent, quas forte viator
     vel nimis admovit vel iam sub luce reliquit,
495   sic deus in flammas abiit, sic pectore toto
     uritur et sterilem sperando nutrit amorem.
     spectat inornatos collo pendere capillos
     et "quid, si comantur?" ait. videt igne micantes
     sideribus similes oculos, videt oscula, quae non
500   est vidisse satis; laudat digitosque manusque
     bracchiaque et nudos media plus parte lacertos;
     si qua latent, meliora putat. fugit ocior aura
     illa levi neque ad haec revocantis verba resistit:
     "nympha, precor, Penei, mane! non insequor hostis;
505   nympha, mane! sic agna lupum, sic cerva leonem,
     sic aquilam penna fugiunt trepidante columbae,
     hostes quaeque suos: amor est mihi causa sequendi!
     me miserum! ne prona cadas indignave laedi
     crura notent sentes et sim tibi causa doloris!
510   aspera, qua properas, loca sunt: moderatius, oro,
     curre fugamque inhibe, moderatius insequar ipse.
     cui placeas, inquire tamen: non incola montis,
     non ego sum pastor, non hic armenta gregesque
     horridus observo. nescis, temeraria, nescis,
515   quem fugias, ideoque fugis: mihi Delphica tellus
     et Claros et Tenedos Patareaque regia servit;
     Iuppiter est genitor; per me, quod eritque fuitque
     estque, patet; per me concordant carmina nervis.
     certa quidem nostra est, nostra tamen una sagitta
520   certior, in vacuo quae vulnera pectore fecit!
     inventum medicina meum est, opiferque per orbem
     dicor, et herbarum subiecta potentia nobis.
     ei mihi, quod nullis amor est sanabilis herbis
     nec prosunt domino, quae prosunt omnibus, artes!"

# Short Answer Questions

Line 493     What is the antecedent of *quas*? **facibus**

Line 498     Translate *comantur*. **"they were arranged"**

              What is the case and use of *igne*? **ablative of means**

Line 500     What type of infinitive is *vidisse*? **perfect active**

              How might it best be translated? **"to have seen"**

Line 502     What is the full form for *qua*? **aliqua**

              What is the expressed subject of *fugit*? **illa (line 503)**

Line 503     What type of participle is *revocantis*? **present active**

              From which verb is it formed? **revocō, -āre, -āvī, -ātum**

              What is its case and use? **genitive of possession (with *verba* and referring to Apollo—*words of him calling back*)**

Line 506     What nouns are subjects of *fugiunt*? Provide line references in parentheses for your Latin choices. **agna (line 505), cerva (line 505), columbae (line 506), hostes (line 507)**

Line 511     What is the person, number, tense, and mood of *curre* and *inhibe*? **second person singular present imperative**

Line 522     What is the person, number, tense, voice, and mood of *dicor*? **first person singular present indicative passive (deponent)**

              Translate *dicor*. **"I am said [to be]/I am called"**

# Multiple Choice Questions *Suggested time: 12 minutes*

1. From lines 488–489, we understand that
   a. Daphne's father will refuse her request
   **b. Daphne's beauty will not allow her to remain a virgin**
   c. Apollo agrees to stop his pursuit
   d. Apollo continues to pursue Daphne

2. The metrical pattern for the first four feet of line 491 is
   **a. dactyl-spondee-dactyl-spondee**
   b. dactyl-dactyl-spondee-dactyl
   c. spondee-spondee-dactyl-dactyl
   d. dactyl-spondee-dactyl-dactyl

3. The intent of the simile in lines 492–494 is to compare the burning of torches and fields to
   a. the heat of the sun driven by Phoebus Apollo
   b. the speed of Apollo's pursuit
   **c. the depth of Apollo's passion**
   d. the countryside through which Apollo and Daphne run

4. In line 493, *ut* is translated
   a. when
   b. in order that
   c. since
   **d. just as**

5. The repeated use of *–que* in lines 500–501 represents which figure of speech?
   a. polyptoton
   b. prolepsis
   **c. polysyndeton**
   d. ellipsis

6. In line 507, *sequendi* is a
   a. gerundive
   **b. gerund**
   c. present participle
   d. present passive infinitive

7. The intent of lines 515–518 is to
   **a. impress Daphne**
   b. impress the reader with Ovid's knowledge
   c. persuade Apollo to stop running
   d. provide solemnity

8. The figure of speech found in lines 517–518 is
   a. prolepsis
   b. personification
   c. zeugma
   **d. polyptoton**

9. In line 519, the case of *una* is
   a. accusative
   b. ablative
   **c. nominative**
   d. dative

10. The best translation of line 523 (*nullis . . . herbis*) is
    **a. love is curable by no plants**
    b. no love is curable with plants
    c. love is curable by all plants
    d. love has cures with plants

# Translation *Suggested time: 15 minutes*

Translate the passage below as literally as possible.

> cui placeas, inquire tamen: non incola montis,
> non ego sum pastor, non hic armenta gregesque
> horridus observo. nescis, temeraria, nescis,
> quem fugias, ideoque fugis: mihi Delphica tellus
> 5     et Claros et Tenedos Patareaque regia servit;
> Iuppiter est genitor; per me, quod eritque fuitque
> estque, patet; per me concordant carmina nervis.

*Metamorphoses 1.512–518*

Nevertheless, ask who it is whom you please: I am not an inhabitant of the mountain, I am not a shepherd, I am not an uncivilized soul who watches over herds and flocks hereabouts. You do not know, rash girl, you do not know from whom you flee, and that is why you flee: the Delphic region and Claros and Tenedos and the Patarean palace serve me; Jupiter is my father; through me what will be and was and is, is revealed; through me do songs harmonize with the strings.

**18 chunks. 9 points total, 1/2 point each. Round up to nearest whole point.**

| | |
|---|---|
| *cui placeas* | **whom you please/to whom you are pleasing** |
| *inquire tamen* | **nevertheless ask** |
| *non incola montis* | **[I am] not an inhabitant of the mountain** |
| *non ego sum pastor* | **I am not a shepherd** |
| *non hic … horridus observo* | **I, not uncivilized, watch over/guard hereabouts/here** |
| *armenta gregesque* | **herds and flocks** |
| *nescis, temeraria, nescis* | **you do not know, rash one, you do not know** |
| *quem fugias* | **whom/from whom you flee** |
| *ideoque fugis* | **and that is the reason you flee** |
| *Delphica tellus et Claros et Tenedos Patareaque regia* | **the Delphic land and Claros and Tenedos and the Patarean palace** |
| *mihi … servit* | **serve me** |
| *Iuppiter est genitor* | **Jupiter is my father/ancestor/begetter** |
| *per me* | **through me** |
| *quod eritque fuitque estque* | **that which will be and was/has been and is** |
| *patet* | **is revealed** |
| *per me* | **through me** |
| *concordant carmina* | **songs harmonize** |
| *nervis* | **with the strings** |

# Short Analysis Questions

1.  How do the phrases *sed te decor iste quod optas/ esse vetat* and *votoque tuo tua forma repugnat* (lines 488–89) raise the level of pathos in this scene?

    **Daphne is powerless in her request. Her fate is doomed by her extraordinary beauty. These phrases are uttered by the narrator, outside Daphne's direct address to her father. What is obvious to others is not recognized by Daphne herself: her beauty, which makes her so attractive to men, will prevent her remaining a virgin although she cannot see that at the moment.**

2.  How does the phrase *suaque illum oracula fallunt* (line 491) raise the level of pathos in this scene?

    **Like Daphne's blindness to her own beauty, Apollo's gift of prophecy, so valuable to others, fails to inform him of what will be.**

3.  Write out and identify a synthesis in lines 502–503.

    **A    B    A    B**
    **Ocior aura illa levi**

4.  To what earlier event is Apollo referring with the words *nostra tamen una sagitta certior* (lines 519–520)?

    **He is referring to Cupid and his one more accurate arrow.**

# Vocabulary

Below you will find a list of high-frequency words you have encountered in your recent readings. For all the words you know, write out full dictionary entries, including English meanings, and put a √ mark in the left-hand column to show you have already committed these words to memory. For any words you do not yet know, write out the dictionary entries using the end glossary and learn them as soon as possible.

√

1.  _____ *aliquis* _____

2.  _____ *ardeō* _____

3.  _____ *cadō* _____

4.  _____ *causa* _____

5.  _____ *collum* _____

6.  _____ *dīcō* _____

7.  _____ *digitus* _____

8. ____ *herba* _____

9. ____ *hostis* _____

10. ____ *iam* _____

11. ____ *laedō* _____

12. ____ *maneō* _____

13. ____ *mors* _____

14. ____ *nervus* _____

15. ____ *nesciō* _____

16. ____ *noster* _____

17. ____ *nympha* _____

18. ____ *omnis* _____

19. ____ *orbis* _____

20. ____ *precor* _____

21. ____ *prōsum* _____

22. ____ *putō* _____

23. ____ *sagitta* _____

24. ____ *tōtus* _____

25. ____ *vacuus* _____

26. ____ *vel* _____

27. ____ *videō* _____

28. ____ *vulnus* _____

# APOLLO AND DAPHNE
# METAMORPHOSES 1.525–567

525     Plura locuturum timido Peneia cursu
fugit cumque ipso verba inperfecta reliquit,
tum quoque visa decens; nudabant corpora venti,
obviaque adversas vibrabant flamina vestes,
et levis inpulsos retro dabat aura capillos,
530     auctaque forma fuga est. sed enim non sustinet ultra
perdere blanditias iuvenis deus, utque monebat
ipse Amor, admisso sequitur vestigia passu.
ut canis in vacuo leporem cum Gallicus arvo
vidit, et hic praedam pedibus petit, ille salutem;
535     alter inhaesuro similis iam iamque tenere
sperat et extento stringit vestigia rostro,
alter in ambiguo est, an sit conprensus, et ipsis
morsibus eripitur tangentiaque ora relinquit:
sic deus et virgo est hic spe celer, illa timore.
540     qui tamen insequitur pennis adiutus Amoris,
ocior est requiemque negat tergoque fugacis
inminet et crinem sparsum cervicibus adflat.
viribus absumptis expalluit illa citaeque
victa labore fugae spectans Peneidas undas
545*    "fer, pater," inquit "opem! si flumina numen habetis,
547     qua nimium placui, mutando perde figuram!"
vix prece finita torpor gravis occupat artus,
mollia cinguntur tenui praecordia libro,
550     in frondem crines, in ramos bracchia crescunt,
pes modo tam velox pigris radicibus haeret,
ora cacumen habet: remanet nitor unus in illa.
       Hanc quoque Phoebus amat positaque in stipite dextra
sentit adhuc trepidare novo sub cortice pectus
555     conplexusque suis ramos ut membra lacertis
oscula dat ligno; refugit tamen oscula lignum.
cui deus "at, quoniam coniunx mea non potes esse,
arbor eris certe" dixit "mea! semper habebunt
te coma, te citharae, te nostrae, laure, pharetrae;
560     tu ducibus Latiis aderis, cum laeta Triumphum

---

* The lack of a line 546 is due to uncertainties and inaccuracies in the ancient texts.

vox canet et visent longas Capitolia pompas;
postibus Augustis eadem fidissima custos
ante fores stabis mediamque tuebere quercum,
utque meum intonsis caput est iuvenale capillis,
565    tu quoque perpetuos semper gere frondis honores!"
finierat Paean: factis modo laurea ramis
adnuit utque caput visa est agitasse cacumen.

## Short Answer Questions

Line 525    Of which verb is *plura* the direct object? **locuturum (est)**

Line 534    What is the antecedent of *hic*? **canis (line 533)**

             What is the antecedent of *ille*? **leporem (line 533)**

Line 535    What is the form of *inhaesuro*? **future active participle**

             What is the case and use of *inhaesuro*? **dative with certain adjectives (*similis*)**

             To whom does *alter* refer? **canis (line 533)**

Line 537    To whom does *alter* refer? **leporem (line 533)**

Line 540    Whom does *adiutus* describe? **Apollo**

Line 541    To whom does *fugacis* refer? **Daphne**

Line 545    What is the form of *fer*? **second person singular present imperative active**

Line 547    What is the form of *mutando*? **gerund**

             What is the case and use of *mutando*? **ablative of means**

Line 559    What is the case of *laure*? **vocative**

Lines 560–561 What is the tense of *aderis, canet,* and *visent*? **future**

Line 566    What grammatical construction do the two words *factis . . . ramis* form? **ablative absolute**

## Multiple Choice Questions *Suggested time: 12 minutes*

1. In lines 525–526, we learn that
   a. Apollo said many things to Daphne
   **b. Daphne fled before Apollo could say many things to her**
   c. Apollo was too shy to speak to Daphne
   d. Daphne said many things to Apollo as she fled

2. Line 528 makes use of
   a. synchesis
   b. assonance
   c. golden line
   **d. all of the above**

3. In line 533, *ut* introduces a(n)
   a. result clause
   b. purpose clause
   **c. simile**
   d. indirect command

4. *perde* in line 547 is a
   **a. second singular imperative verb**
   b. first singular present tense subjunctive verb
   c. first singular future tense indicative verb
   d. third singular present tense indicative verb

5. The most literal translation for *vix prece finita* in line 548 is
   a. having hardly finished her prayer
   b. hardly finishing her prayer
   **c. her prayer hardly having been finished**
   d. her prayer hardly finishing

6. The best translation for line 555 (*complexus . . . lacertis*) is
   **a. having embraced with his arms her branches as though limbs**
   b. having embraced her arms with his limbs as branches
   c. having been embraced with her arms as limbs
   d. her branches having been embraced as limbs with his arms

7. In line 556, we learn that
   a. Daphne welcomes his kisses
   b. Daphne returns his kisses
   c. Apollo shuns Daphne's kisses
   **d. Daphne recoils from his kisses**

8. Lines 560–561 refer to the future duties of the laurel/bay at
   a. weddings
   b. civic ceremonies
   c. legal proceedings
   **d. military ceremonies**

9. The best translation for line 564 (*utque . . . capillis*) is

a. in order for my youthful head to be unshaven

b. **as my head is youthful with unshaven hair**

c. as my head is unshaven with youthful hair

d. so that my head remain youthful with unshaven hair

10. The metrical pattern of the first four feet of line 567 is

a. dactyl-dactyl-dactyl-dactyl

b. dactyl-dactyl-dactyl-spondee

c. dactyl-spondee-dactyl-dactyl

d. **dactyl-dactyl-spondee-dactyl**

## Translation *Suggested time: 15 minutes*

Translate the passage below as literally as possible.

> ut canis in vacuo leporem cum Gallicus arvo
> vidit, et hic praedam pedibus petit, ille salutem;
> alter inhaesuro similis iam iamque tenere
> sperat et extento stringit vestigia rostro,
> 5   alter in ambiguo est, an sit conprensus, et ipsis
> morsibus eripitur tangentiaque ora relinquit:
> sic deus et virgo est hic spe celer, illa timore.

*Metamorphoses 1.533–539*

Just as when the Gallic hound has seen a hare in an empty field, he seeks his prey with his feet and the hare seeks safety; the hound, similar to one who is about to grasp, hopes to catch [it/the hare] at any minute and grazes the soles of its feet with his muzzle thrust forward, the other one [the hare] is uncertain whether it has been caught or not, and snatches itself away from the very bites and leaves behind the mouth just touching it: thus are the god and maiden, he, swift from hope, she, from fear.

**18 chunks. 9 points total, 1/2 point each. Round up to nearest whole point.**

| | |
|---|---|
| *ut canis . . . cum Gallicus* | **just as when the Gallic hound/dog** |
| *vidit* | **has seen** |
| *leporem* | **a hare** |
| *in vacuo . . . arvo* | **in and empty field** |
| *et hic praedam pedibus petit* | **and he seeks his prey with his feet** |
| *ille salutem* | **the hare/that one (seeks) his safety** |
| *alter inhaesuro similis* | **the one (hound) similar to one about to grasp** |
| *iam iamque tenere sperat* | **hopes to hold onto it at that very moment** |
| *et . . . stringit vestigia* | **and grazes the soles of its feet** |
| *extento . . . rostro* | **with its thrust forward/outstretched muzzle** |
| *alter in ambiguo est* | **the other one (hare) is uncertain** |
| *an sit conprensus* | **whether it has been caught or not** |
| *et eripitur* | **and snatches itself away from** |

| ipsis morsibus | the very bites/bitings |
| tangentiaque ora relinquit | and leaves behind the mouth just touching |
| sic deus et virgo est | thus (are) the god and the maiden |
| hic spe celer | he swift with/from hope |
| illa timore | she with/from fear |

# Short Analysis Questions

1. a. Write out and identify a synthesis in line 529.

   | **A** | **B** | **A** | **B** |
   | **levis** | **inpulsos** | **aura** | **capillos** |

   b. Briefly explain its possible effect on the meaning of the line.

   **The synthesis mimics the motion of the wind blowing her hair back and forth.**

2. Cite the Latin that incorporates two antonyms in line 551 and briefly examine their effect on the line.

   **In line 551 *velox* and *pigris* are antonyms and graphically represent the change in Daphne from a swift-footed runner to a tree with its roots anchored to the ground.**

3. Briefly discuss the effect of the tricolon crescendo on line 559.

   **Setting each element of the tricolon crescendo off with anaphora, Ovid highlights those attributes of Apollo which are most well-known and which will always be reminiscent of Daphne.**

# Essay *Suggested time: 20 minutes*

In this first erotic tale of the *Metamorphoses*, Ovid juxtaposes two motifs: hunting and sexual passion. These manifest themselves at times as hunter and lover and at other times as hunter and hunted. In a short essay explore these seemingly opposing roles. Where do they show up together in the same character and when do they belong only to Apollo or Daphne? Do the characters ever reverse their roles?

Support your assertions with references drawn from **throughout** lines 452–567. All Latin words must be copied or their line numbers provided, AND they must be translated or paraphrased closely enough so that it is clear you understand the Latin. It is your responsibility to convince your reader that you are basing your conclusions on the Latin text and not merely on a general recollection of the passage. Direct your answer to the question; do not merely summarize the passage. Please write your essay on a separate piece of paper.

**The question asks students to examine how the poet suggests that the equation of hunting and sexual passion is both traditional and highly problematical. Students should refer to specific passages (lines 474–487) and (lines 504–524) where Apollo and Daphne are depicted. The grader should look for an argument that shows the role reversals (transformations) in the story: Apollo is a glorious hunter who has killed the Python; he is transformed into comical lover; while Daphne, virgin huntress who rejects love, becomes the hunted prey, a victim whose transformation into a tree is ambiguous at best.**

6 – A fully developed essay that recognizes the problematical nature of equating hunting and sexual passion and that selects Latin passages as evidence for how Apollo and Daphne are both transformed by this equation. The student understands the entire passage and chooses correctly cited Latin to support his assertions. The discussion is coherent and of high quality.

5 – A strong essay with good analysis, but one which is not fully developed. The student has formulated a good argument that shows the complexity of the hunter/sexual passion equation. Latin is correctly cited.

4 – A competent response, but one which does not fully see the complexity of the roles of both Daphne and Apollo. The discussion is more descriptive than analytical. Latin support is not extensive.

3 – A less competent response that uses inappropriate Latin passages and is not truly analytical. A 3 paper may also respond well to the question but fails to cite any Latin passages.

2 – An essay that is too general and vague, though it reveals some understanding of the passage. The Latin cited indicates little comprehension.

1 – A response that is incoherent, in spite of including some relevant information. The student does not appear to have a real understanding of the passage.

0 – The response is irrelevant to the topic or incorrect, or merely restates the question without any analysis.

## Scansion

Scan the following lines.

inventum medicina me(um) est, opiferque per orbem

dicor, et herbarum subiecta potentia nobis.

ei mihi, quod nullis amor est sanabilis herbis

nec prosunt domino, quae prosunt omnibus, artes!"

*Metamorphoses 1.521–524*

# Vocabulary

Below you will find a list of high-frequency words you have encountered in your recent readings. For all the words you know, write out full dictionary entries, including English meanings, and put a √ mark in the left-hand column to show you have already committed these words to memory. For any words you do not yet know, write out the dictionary entries using the end glossary and learn them as soon as possible.

√

1. _____ *adsum* _____

2. _____ *an* _____

3. _____ *arbor* _____

4. _____ *arvum* _____

5. _____ *aura* _____

6. _____ *blanditia* _____

7. _____ *caput* _____

8. _____ *cervix* _____

9. _____ *deus* _____

10. _____ *fīdus* _____

11. _____ *forma* _____

12. _____ *frons* _____

13. _____ *fuga* _____

14. _____ *fugiō* _____

15. _____ *gerō* _____

16. _____ *ipse* _____

17. _____ *lacertus* _____

18. _____ *levis* _____

19. _____ *medius* _____

20. _____ *nūdus* _____

21. _____ *pectus* _____

22. ____ *penna* _____

23. ____ *placeō* _____

24. ____ *sed* _____

25. ____ *sequor* _____

26. ____ *sīc* _____

27. ____ *spectō* _____

28. ____ *sub* _____

29. ____ *tamen* _____

30. ____ *ūnus* _____

31. ____ *ut* _____

# PYRAMUS AND THISBE
# METAMORPHOSES 4.55–92

55 "Pyramus et Thisbe, iuvenum pulcherrimus alter,
  altera, quas Oriens habuit, praelata puellis,
  contiguas tenuere domos, ubi dicitur altam
  coctilibus muris cinxisse Semiramis urbem.
  notitiam primosque gradus vicinia fecit,
60 tempore crevit amor; taedae quoque iure coissent,
  sed vetuere patres; quod non potuere vetare,
  ex aequo captis ardebant mentibus ambo.
  conscius omnis abest, nutu signisque loquuntur,
  quoque magis tegitur, tectus magis aestuat ignis.
65 fissus erat tenui rima, quam duxerat olim,
  cum fieret, paries domui communis utrique.
  id vitium nulli per saecula longa notatum—
  quid non sentit amor?—primi vidistis amantes
  et vocis fecistis iter, tutaeque per illud
70 murmure blanditiae minimo transire solebant.
  saepe, ubi constiterant hinc Thisbe, Pyramus illinc,
  inque vices fuerat captatus anhelitus oris,
  'invide' dicebant 'paries, quid amantibus obstas?
  quantum erat, ut sineres toto nos corpore iungi,
75 aut, hoc si nimium est, vel ad oscula danda pateres?
  nec sumus ingrati: tibi nos debere fatemur,
  quod datus est verbis ad amicas transitus auris.'
  talia diversa nequiquam sede locuti
  sub noctem dixere 'vale' partique dedere
80 oscula quisque suae non pervenientia contra.
  postera nocturnos Aurora removerat ignes,
  solque pruinosas radiis siccaverat herbas:
  ad solitum coiere locum. tum murmure parvo
  multa prius questi statuunt, ut nocte silenti
85 fallere custodes foribusque excedere temptent,
  cumque domo exierint, urbis quoque tecta relinquant,
  neve sit errandum lato spatiantibus arvo,
  conveniant ad busta Nini lateantque sub umbra
  arboris: arbor ibi niveis uberrima pomis,
90 ardua morus, erat, gelido contermina fonti.
  pacta placent; et lux, tarde discedere visa,
  praecipitatur aquis, et aquis nox exit ab isdem.

# Short Answer Questions

Line 56     What is the form of *praelata*? **perfect passive participle**

           What is its first principal part? ***praefero***

           What word does *praelata* modify? ***altera* (Thisbe)**

Line 58     What is the case and use of *coctilibus muris*? **ablative of means**

Line 65     What is the form of *fissus*? **perfect passive participle (of *findo*)**

           What word does *fissus* modify? ***paries***

Line 66     What is the mood and reason for *fieret*? **subjunctive, *cum* circumstantial clause**

           What is the case and use of *domui*? **dative with certain adjectives (*communis*)**

Line 68     What is the form of *amantes*? **present active participle**

           What word does *amantes* modify? **you (pl.) *vidistis* (line 68) and *fecistis* (line 69)**

Line 69     What is the case and use of *vocis*? **objective genitive**

Line 74     What is the mood and reason for *sineres*? **subjunctive, consecutive/result clause**

           What is the form of *iungi*? **present passive infinitive**

           How is this form used? **indirect statement**

Line 80     What is the form of *pervenientia*? **present active participle**

           What does *pervenientia* modify? ***oscula***

Line 82     What is the case and use of *radiis*? **ablative of means**

Line 83     What is the form of *coiere*? **third person plural perfect indicative active (of *coeo*); alternate form for *coierunt***

Line 86     What is the case and use of *domo*? **ablative of separation/place from which**

           What is the form of *exierint*? **third person plural perfect subjunctive active (of *exeo*)**

           How is this form used? ***cum* circumstantial clause**

Line 88     What is the form of *conveniant*? **present subjunctive active (purpose clause)**

# Multiple Choice Questions *Suggested time: 12 minutes*

1. The antecedent to *quas* in line 56 is
   a. *altera* (line 56)
   b. *Oriens* (line 56)
   **c. *puellis* (line 56)**
   d. *Thisbe* (line 55)

2. The metrical pattern of the first four feet of line 58 is
   a. spondee-dactyl-spondee-dactyl
   **b. dactyl-spondee-spondee-dactyl**
   c. dactyl-spondee-dactyl-spondee
   d. dactyl-dactyl-spondee-spondee

3. What figure of speech is employed in line 64?
   a. hyperbaton
   b. irony
   c. anaphora
   **d. polyptoton**

4. Whom is the poet addressing in line 68, *quid non sentit amor?*
   a. the lovers
   b. their parents
   c. the wall
   **d. his general audience**

5. In line 81, *nocturnos . . . ignes* are
   **a. stars**
   b. campfires
   c. the fires of love
   d. hearth fires

6. In line 85, the *custodes* are
   a. guards
   b. servants
   c. parents
   **d. all of the above**

7. *tecta*, in line 86, is an example of
   a. metonymy
   **b. synecdoche**
   c. personification
   d. simile

8. In line 87, *neve sit errandum . . . spatiantibus*, is best translated
   a. so that they should not make a mistake while wandering
   **b. so that there would not be a wandering about for those walking**
   c. so that it must not be wandered by those walking about
   d. so that they did not walk about wandering.

9. *conveniant* in line 88 is a subjunctive in a
   **a. purpose clause**
   b. consecutive clause
   c. relative clause of characteristic
   d. temporal clause

10. The best translation for line 92 (*praecipitatur . . . isdem*) is

   **a. it (the light) sinks into the waters, and
      night goes out from the same waters**

   b. it (the light) is sunk into the water, and
      the night exits from the same water

   c. it (the light) dives into waters, and the
      waters come out in the same night

   d. the sun goes down, into the water, and
      night comes up all the same

## Translation *Suggested time: 15 minutes*

Translate the passage below as literally as possible.

> "Pyramus et Thisbe, iuvenum pulcherrimus alter,
> altera, quas Oriens habuit, praelata puellis,
> contiguas tenuere domos, ubi dicitur altam
> coctilibus muris cinxisse Semiramis urbem.
> 5    notitiam primosque gradus vicinia fecit,
> tempore crevit amor; taedae quoque iure coissent,
> sed vetuere patres; quod non potuere vetare,
> ex aequo captis ardebant mentibus ambo.

*Metamorphoses 4.55–62*

**"Pyramus and Thisbe, he the most handsome of youths, she, most esteemed of the girls whom the Orient held, had neighboring houses at the spot where Semiramis is said to have girded the high city with walls of baked bricks. Proximity brought about the first steps of acquaintance; their love grew in time; marriage torches would then have joined them by law, but their parents forbade it; but what they could not forbid: both burned equally with captured minds.**

**18 chunks. 9 points total, 1/2 point each. Round up to nearest whole point.**

| | |
|---|---|
| *Pyramus et Thisbe* | **Pyramus and Thisbe** |
| *iuvenum pulcherrimus alter* | **the one(he), the most handsome of youths** |
| *altera praelata puellis* | **the other (she), more esteemed among the girls** |
| *quas Oriens habuit* | **whom the Orient (East) held** |
| *contiguas tenuere domos* | **had adjacent houses** |
| *ubi Semiramis dicitur* | **where Semiramis is said** |
| *cinxisse urbem altam* | **to have girded the high city** |
| *coctilibus muris* | **with walls of bricks** |
| *vicinia fecit* | **(their) proximity brought about (made)** |
| *notiam primosque gradus* | **(their) acquaintance and (their) first steps** |
| *tempore crevit amor* | **love grew in time** |
| *quoque coissent taedae* | **also wedding torches would have joined them** |
| *iure* | **by law/custom** |
| *sed vetuere patres* | **but their parents forbade (it)** |
| *quod non potuere vetare* | **what they could not (were not able to) forbid** |
| *ex aequo* | **(was that) equally** |
| *ardebant ambo* | **both burned** |
| *captis mentibus* | **with captured minds** |

# Short Analysis Questions

1.  a.  Lines 69–70 contain an example of what figure of speech?

    **interlocked word order, synchesis (*tutae . . . murmure blanditiae minimo*)**

    b.  Why is this figure particularly appropriate for the situation of Pyramus and Thisbe?

    **Just as the nouns and adjectives are interlocked, so the two lovers are locked together by their mutual love.**

2.  Briefly describe the effect of the direct address in lines 73–77.

    **By addressing the wall, the lovers try to make the wall their friend so that it will allow them to hear each other better, and even to kiss. It makes us, the readers, present as well and thus heightens the pathos.**

3.  a.  Write out a literal translation of *conveniant ad busta Nini, lateantque sub umbra/arboris* (lines 88–89).

    **"They would meet at the tomb of Ninus, and they would take refuge in the shade of a tree."**

    b.  Comment on how these lines foreshadow the outcome of the lovers' plan

    **Both the tomb and the shade of the tree provide ominous signals of death.**

# PYRAMUS AND THISBE
# METAMORPHOSES 4.93–127

"Callida per tenebras versato cardine Thisbe
egreditur fallitque suos adopertaque vultum
95    pervenit ad tumulum dictaque sub arbore sedit
audacem faciebat amor. venit ecce recenti
caede leaena boum spumantis oblita rictus,
depositura sitim vicini fontis in unda;
quam procul ad lunae radios Babylonia Thisbe
100   vidit et obscurum timido pede fugit in antrum,
dumque fugit, tergo velamina lapsa reliquit.
ut lea saeva sitim multa conpescuit unda,
dum redit in silvas, inventos forte sine ipsa
ore cruentato tenues laniavit amictus.
105   serius egressus vestigia vidit in alto
pulvere certa ferae totoque expalluit ore
Pyramus; ut vero vestem quoque sanguine tinctam
repperit, 'una duos' inquit 'nox perdet amantes,
e quibus illa fuit longa dignissima vita;
110   nostra nocens anima est. ego te, miseranda, peremi,
in loca plena metus qui iussi nocte venires
nec prior huc veni. nostrum divellite corpus
et scelerata fero consumite viscera morsu,
o quicumque sub hac habitatis rupe leones!
115   sed timidi est optare necem. 'velamina Thisbes
tollit et ad pactae secum fert arboris umbram,
utque dedit notae lacrimas, dedit oscula vesti,
'accipe nunc' inquit 'nostri quoque sanguinis haustus!'
quoque erat accinctus, demisit in ilia ferrum,
120   nec mora, ferventi moriens e vulnere traxit.
ut iacuit resupinus humo, cruor emicat alte,
non aliter quam cum vitiato fistula plumbo
scinditur et tenui stridente foramine longas
eiaculatur aquas atque ictibus aera rumpit.
125   arborei fetus adspergine caedis in atram
vertuntur faciem, madefactaque sanguine radix
purpureo tinguit pendentia mora colore.

# Short Answer Questions

Line 93    What is the case and use of *versato cardine?* **ablative absolute**

Line 94    What is the case and use of *vultum?* **accusative of specification/respect**

Line 97    What is the case of *oblita?* **nominative**

              What word does *oblita* modify? ***leaena***

              What is the case and use of *rictus?* **accusative of specification/respect**

Line 101    What is the case and number of *lapsa?* **accusative plural**

              What word does *lapsa* modify? ***velamina***

Line 103    Translate *sine ipsa.* **without (Thisbe) herself [in it]**

              Although commonly thought of as an adverb, *forte* is actually the ablative form of which noun? **fors**

Line 110    What is the case of *miseranda?* **vocative**

Line 111    What is the form of *venires?* **second person singular imperfect subjunctive active**

              How is this form used? **indirect command**

Line 115    What is the form of *optare?* **present active infinitive (of *opto*)**

              How is this form used? **verbal noun subject/subject of *est***

Line 118    What is the form of *accipe?* **present imperative active singular**

              Whom is Pyramus addressing? **the robe (*vesti*, line 117)**

Line 120    What is the form of *moriens?* **present active participle (of *morior*)**

              What does *moriens* modify? **he (Pyramus—subject of *traxit* and *demisit*)**

Line 121    What is the case and use of *humo?* **ablative of place where**

# Multiple Choice Questions *Suggested time: 12 minutes*

1. Line 95 (*pervenit . . . sedit*) is best translated as
   a. she arrives at the appointed tomb and sits under a tree
   b. she comes to the tomb and the tree having been appointed, she sits
   **c. she arrives at the tomb and sits under the appointed tree**
   d. the tomb having been appointed, she sits under the tree

2. In lines 96–97, we learn that
   a. a lion has a bloody mouth from a recent kill
   **b. a lioness arrives, her mouth besmeared with blood from a recent kill of cattle**
   c. there has been a recent slaughter of a lioness near the tomb
   d. a lioness arrives famished at the tomb of Ninus

3. What figure of speech is used in line 100?
   **a. chiasmus**
   b. hyperbaton
   c. litotes
   d. hyperbole

4. How does the position of *Pyramus* in lines 105–107 at the end of the clause contribute to the meaning of the lines?
   a. it shows how important he is as a lover
   **b. it reinforces the fact that he is late**
   c. it emphasizes his pallor
   d. it heightens suspense

5. What is the metrical pattern for the first four feet of line 108?
   a. dactyl-spondee-dactyl-spondee
   b. spondee-dactyl-spondee-dactyl
   c. spondee-spondee-dactyl-spondee
   **d. dactyl-dactyl-spondee-spondee**

6. How does the word order in line 108 reinforce the line's meaning?
   a. it shows how quickly one's fortunes can change
   b. it emphasizes that there were two lovers
   **c. it interlocks the fate of the two lovers**
   d. it shows the power of night

7. Whom is Pyramus addressing in line 112?
   a. *custodes* (line 85)
   b. Thisbe
   **c. any lions in the cave**
   d. the lioness

8. Why does Pyramus call his *"viscera scelerata"* in line 113?
   **a. because he feels guilty for coming too late**
   b. because he thinks Thisbe is dead
   c. because he deceived his parents
   d. because he wants the lions to eat him

9. The metrical pattern of the first four feet of line 121 is

   a. dactyl-spondee-dactyl-dactyl

   **c. dactyl-dactyl-dactyl-dactyl**

   b. dactyl-spondee-spondee-dactyl

   d. spondee-spondee-dactyl-dactyl

10. Lines 125–127 describe

    a. the death of Pyramus

    c. the color of Pyramus' blood

    b. the death of the mulberry tree

    **d. the cause of the mulberries' dark color**

## Translation *Suggested time: 15 minutes*

Translate the passage below as literally as possible.

> ut lea saeva sitim multa conpescuit unda,
> dum redit in silvas, inventos forte sine ipsa
> ore cruentato tenues laniavit amictus.
> serius egressus vestigia vidit in alto
> 5    pulvere certa ferae totoque expalluit ore
> Pyramus; ut vero vestem quoque sanguine tinctam
> repperit, 'una duos' inquit 'nox perdet amantes,
> e quibus illa fuit longa dignissima vita;
>
> *Metamorphoses 4.103–109*

When the savage lioness had quenched her thirst with much water and while she returned to the forest, she tore with her blood-stained mouth the thin cloak, having been found by chance, without its mistress herself in it.

Having left too late, Pyramus saw the sure footprints of the wild animal in the deep dust and turned pale over all his face; when truly he discovered too the garment dyed with blood, he said, 'One night will destroy two lovers, of whom she was most worthy of a long life.

18 chunks. 9 points total, 1/2 point each. Round up to nearest whole point.

| | |
|---|---|
| *ut lea saeva* | **When the savage lioness** |
| *sitim conpescuit* | **quenched/had quenched her thirst** |
| *multa unda* | **with much water** |
| *dum redit in silvas* | **while she returned into the forest** |
| *inventos forte tenues amictus* | **the thin cloak discovered/found by chance** |
| *sine ipsa* | **without its mistress/Thisbe herself** |
| *ore cruentato laniavit* | **she tore with her bloodstained mouth** |
| *serius egressus Pyramus* | **Pyramus, having left too late/later** |
| *vestigia vidit certa ferae* | **saw the sure footprints of the wild animal** |
| *in alto pulvere* | **in the deep dust** |
| *totoque expalluit ore* | **and he grew pale all over his/over his whole face** |
| *ut vero vestem quoque repperit* | **when truly he also discovered/found the garment** |

| | |
|---|---|
| *sanguine tinctam* | **dyed with blood** |
| *inquit* | **he said** |
| *una duos nox perdet amantes* | **one night will destroy two lovers** |
| *e quibus* | **of/from whom** |
| *illa fuit dignissima* | **she was most worthy/worthiest** |
| *longa vita* | **of a long life** |

# Short Analysis Questions

1.  a.  Translate *nostra nocens anima est/ ego te, miseranda, peremi* (line 110).

    **"My soul is guilty. I have killed you, you who must be pitied."**

    b.  What is the effect of the juxtaposition of the words *ego te* (line 110)?

    **The *ego te* juxtaposition illustrates the closeness or the inseparability of the two lovers.**

    c.  What is the effect of the apostrophe *miseranda* (line 110)?

    **Believing her to be dead, Pyramus addresses Thisbe as if she were alive, adding to the pathos of his situation.**

2.  a.  Translate *sed timidi est optare necem* (line 115).

    **"But to wish for death is for the timid."**

    b.  Explain what this typical Roman maxim means in the context of this passage.

    **The brave man does not <u>wish</u> for death. He takes immediate action and kills himself.**

3.  a.  To what does the poet compare Pyramus' wound in lines 122–124?

    **a broken lead pipe**

    b.  Which figure of speech does this simile employ?

    **hyperbole**

4.  Lines 125–127 describe a metamorphosis.

    a.  What is transformed?

    **The fruit of the mulberry tree becomes purple.**

    b.  What was the original color of the fruit?

    **white**

# PYRAMUS AND THISBE
# METAMORPHOSES 4.128–166

"Ecce metu nondum posito, ne fallat amantem,
illa redit iuvenemque oculis animoque requirit,
130    quantaque vitarit narrare pericula gestit;
utque locum et visa cognoscit in arbore formam,
sic facit incertam pomi color: haeret, an haec sit.
dum dubitat, tremebunda videt pulsare cruentum
membra solum, retroque pedem tulit, oraque buxo
135    pallidiora gerens exhorruit aequoris instar,
quod tremit, exigua cum summum stringitur aura.
sed postquam remorata suos cognovit amores,
percutit indignos claro plangore lacertos
et laniata comas amplexaque corpus amatum
140    vulnera supplevit lacrimis fletumque cruori
miscuit et gelidis in vultibus oscula figens
'Pyrame,' clamavit, 'quis te mihi casus ademit?
Pyrame, responde! tua te carissima Thisbe
nominat; exaudi vultusque attolle iacentes!'
145    ad nomen Thisbes oculos a morte gravatos
Pyramus erexit visaque recondidit illa.

"Quae postquam vestemque suam cognovit et ense
vidit ebur vacuum, 'tua te manus' inquit 'amorque
perdidit, infelix! est et mihi fortis in unum
150    hoc manus, est et amor: dabit hic in vulnera vires.
persequar extinctum letique miserrima dicar
causa comesque tui: quique a me morte revelli
heu sola poteras, poteris nec morte revelli.
hoc tamen amborum verbis estote rogati,
155    o multum miseri meus illiusque parentes,
ut, quos certus amor, quos hora novissima iunxit,
conponi tumulo non invideatis eodem;
at tu, quae ramis arbor miserabile corpus
nunc tegis unius, mox es tectura duorum,
160    signa tene caedis pullosque et luctibus aptos
semper habe fetus, gemini monimenta cruoris.'
dixit et aptato pectus mucrone sub imum
incubuit ferro, quod adhuc a caede tepebat.
vota tamen tetigere deos, tetigere parentes:
165    nam color in pomo est, ubi permaturuit, ater,
quodque rogis superest, una requiescit in urna."

# Short Answer Questions

Line 128    What is the construction of *metu nondum posito?* **ablative absolute**

Translate the construction. **"though her fear was not yet cast off"**

What is the form of *fallat?* **third person singular present subjunctive active**

How is this form used? **negative purpose clause**

Line 129    What is the case and use of *oculis?* **ablative of means**

Line 130    What is the form of *vitarit?* **third person singular perfect subjunctive active (contracted from *vitaverit*)**

How is this form used? **indirect question**

Line 131    What is the form of *visa?* **perfect passive participle (of *video*)**

Translate *visa.* **"having been seen (with *arbore*); which was seen (which she saw)"**

Line 135    What is the case and use of *aequoris?* **genitive, with *instar***

Line 139    What is the form of *laniata?* **perfect passive participle (from *lanio*)**

What word does *laniata* modify? **illa (subject of *percutit*, line 138, and *supplevit*, line 140)**

Translate *laniata.* **"having been torn"**

What is the case and use of *comas?* **accusative of specification/specification (a Greek usage)**

Line 140    What is the case and use of *cruori?* **dative, with *miscuit* (line 141)**

Line 145    What is the case and use of *morte?* **ablative of means**

Line 152    What is the form of *revelli?* **present infinitive passive**

How is this form used? **complementary (with *poteras,* line 153)**

Line 157    What is the form of *invideatis?* **second person plural present subjunctive active**

How is this form used? **indirect command**

# Multiple Choice Questions *Suggested time: 12 minutes*

1.  In line 129, *oculis animoque requirit* is an example of which figure of speech?
    a.  hyperbole
    b.  hendiadys
    **c.  zeugma**
    d.  hysteron proteron

2. The metrical pattern of the first four feet of line 132 is
   a. dactyl-dactyl-spondee-spondee
   b. dactyl-spondee-dactyl-spondee
   **c. dactyl-spondee-spondee-dactyl**
   d. spondee-dactyl-spondee-dactyl

3. In lines 132–134, Thisbe becomes fearful because
   a. she isn't sure she is in the right place
   b. she sees that the color of the berries has changed
   c. she sees Pyramus' trembling limbs beating the ground
   **d. all of the above**

4. *buxo* in line 134 is an ablative of
   a. means
   b. manner
   c. agent
   **d. comparison**

5. In line 138, *indignos . . . lacertos* is an example of
   a. a metaphor
   b. a simile
   c. hyperbole
   **d. personification**

6. Line 142 (*'Pyrame,' . . . ademit?*) is best translated
   a. Pyramus called, who has taken away from me your accident?
   **b. Pyramus, she called, what accident has taken you from me?**
   c. Pyramus, she called, who has taken you from me by accident?
   d. Pyramus shouted who has taken you away from me?

7. In lines 149–150, we learn that Thisbe
   a. has a brave hand
   b. has brave love
   **c. has decided to kill herself**
   d. is strong

8. The case of *sola* (line 153) is
   a. nominative singular
   b. neuter plural
   c. vocative singular
   **d. ablative singular**

9. In line 157, Thisbe addresses
   a. Pyramus
   **b. their fathers**
   c. the tree
   d. the tomb

10. The antecedent to *quod* (line 166) is
    a. *ater* (line 165)
    b. *color* (line 165)
    **c. id (understood)**
    d. *pomo* (line 165)

## Translation *Suggested time: 15 minutes*

Translate the passage below as literally as possible.

> o multum miseri meus illiusque parentes,
> ut, quos certus amor, quos hora novissima iunxit,
> conponi tumulo non invideatis eodem;
> at tu, quae ramis arbor miserabile corpus
> 5     nunc tegis unius, mox es tectura duorum,
> signa tene caedis pullosque et luctibus aptos
> semper habe fetus, gemini monimenta cruoris.'
>
>              *Metamorphoses 4.155–161*

**Oh much wretched parents of me and of him, do not refuse that those whom true love, whom the very last hour joined, be put in the same tomb. But you, tree, who now with your branches cover the pitiful corpse of one, are soon going to cover two, hold onto the signs of this slaughter and always have fruit both somber and suitable for grief, memorials of twin bloodshed.**

**18 chunks. 9 points total, 1/2 point each. Round up to nearest whole point.**

| | |
|---|---|
| *o multum miseri* | **oh much/very wretched** |
| *meus illiusque parentes* | **parents of me and of him** |
| *ut non invideatis* | **do not refuse** |
| *quos certus amor* | **that those whom certain love** |
| *quos hora novissima iunxit* | **whom the very last/most recent hour has joined** |
| *conponi tumulo eodem* | **be placed together in the same tomb** |
| *at tu arbor* | **while you, tree,** |
| *quae nunc* | **who now** |
| *tegis ramis* | **cover with your branches** |
| *miserabile corpus* | **the wretched/pitiful body** |
| *unius mox duorum* | **of one, soon of two** |
| *es tectura* | **are about to/going to (will) cover** |
| *signa tene caedis* | **hold onto the signs of this slaughter** |
| *et semper habe* | **and always have** |
| *pullosque aptos fetus* | **fruits both somber and suitable for** |
| *luctibus* | **mournings/grief** |
| *monimenta* | **memorials** |
| *gemini cruoris* | **of this twin bloodshed** |

## Short Analysis Questions

1.   a.  Translate *quantaque vitarit narrare pericula gestit* (line 130).

      **"She wanted to tell what great dangers she avoided."**

    b.  Why is this line both pathetic and ironic?

      **It is pathetic because she cannot tell Pyramus what has happened since he is dead. It is ironic because the greatest dangers lie ahead—the death of both lovers.**

2.  a.  To what does Ovid compare Thisbe's shudder in lines 135–136?

    **water struck by a light breeze**

    b.  How appropriate is this simile as a way of illustrating Thisbe's fear and horror?

    **The simile makes Thisbe's shudder visible, yet understates her fear by deemphasizing it with litotes (*exigua . . . aura*.)**

3.  In lines 138–141, Ovid describes Thisbe's gestures of mourning. Delineate six ways that Thisbe mourns. Give the Latin for each action and translate it loosely.

    a.  *claro plangore*—**she laments**

    b.  *percutit lacertos*—**she beats her arms**

    c.  *laniata comas*—**she tears her hair**

    d.  *amplexaque corpus*—**she embraces the body (of her lover)**

    e.  *vulnera supplevit lacrimis*—**she fills his wounds with tears;** *fletumque cruori miscuit*—**she mingles her tears with his blood**

    f.  *in vultibus oscula figens*—**she kisses his face**

## Essay *Suggested time: 20 minutes*

Pyramus and Thisbe is a tragic love story. In lines 110–112, Pyramus blames himself for Thisbe's death. Yet, the poet suggests other reasons for the tragic outcome. Write an essay in which you discuss what you believe are the major causes of the tragedy.

Support your assertions with references drawn from **throughout** lines 55–166. All Latin words must be copied or their line numbers provided, AND they must be translated or paraphrased closely enough so that it is clear you understand the Latin. It is your responsibility to convince your reader that you are basing your conclusions on the Latin text and not merely on a general recollection of the passage. Direct your answer to the question; do not merely summarize the passage. Please write your essay on a separate piece of paper.

**The question asks students to look beyond Pyramus's self-blame to other causes of the tragic deaths of the lovers. Students should formulate an argument that indicates the cause or causes of the tragedy. Passages that they might choose include (60–61; 84–93; 100–104; 110–115; 147–153). Students might choose to blame the parents of the victims, chance, misapprehension; they might well argue that Pyramus's lateness was also a cause of the unfortunate deaths.**

**6 – A fully developed essay which discusses the major causes of the tragedy. The student makes ample reference to specific aspects of the Latin text to support his analysis and his position. Latin references are properly cited. Even though there may be occasional mistakes, the discussion is coherent and of high quality.**

5 – A strong essay which discusses the major causes of the tragedy. Although the piece has good analysis, it is not so fully developed nor so supported with references to the text as a 6 paper. Latin references are properly cited. The essay reflects familiarity with the poem.

4 – A competent response which discusses the major causes of the tragedy. There may be uneven development. Although limited in quantity, the essay includes accurate and relevant references in responding to the topic. The discussion may be more descriptive than analytical.

3 – A limited response which discusses the major causes of the tragedy. The Latin support is weak and/or inappropriate. Latin references are not properly cited. The answer is descriptive as opposed to analytical. In some 3 papers, the student demonstrates an understanding of the poem but cites no Latin to support his answer.

2 – Some understanding of the poem, but the essay is general and/or vague. The discussion is flawed. The Latin cited demonstrates very limited comprehension.

1 – An incoherent response. While it does contain some relevant information, no substantive argument is presented. The student demonstrates no understanding of the poem.

0 – A response that is off-topic, completely incorrect, or irrelevant. Responses that merely restate the question are also a 0.

# Scansion

Scan the following lines.

$$\_ \;\; \cup\cup\_ \;\; \cup \;\; \cup \;\_ \;\; \cup \;\; \cup \;\_ \;\_ \;\_\cup \;\; \cup\_ \;\_$$
dum dubitat, tremebunda videt pulsare cruentum

$$\_ \;\; \cup \;\; \cup \;\_ \;\_ \;\_ \;\; \cup \;\; \cup \;\_ \;\; \cup\cup \;\_\cup \;\; \cup \;\_ \;\_$$
membra solum, retroque pedem tulit, oraque buxo

$$\_ \;\; \cup\cup\_\cup \;\; \cup \;\_ \;\_ \;\_ \;\; \cup\cup \;\_ \;\; \cup\cup \;\_ \;\_$$
pallidiora gerens exhorruit aequoris instar,

$$\_ \;\; \cup \;\; \cup \;\_\cup\cup\_ \;\_ \;\_ \;\_ \;\_ \;\; \cup\cup \;\_ \;\_$$
quod tremit, exigua cum summum stringitur aura.

*Metamorphoses 4.133–136*

# Vocabulary

1.  Give the positive and comparative forms for *pulcherrimus* (line 55) and the meanings for each.

    a.  *pulcher*                          **beautiful**

    b.  *pulchrior*                        **more beautiful**

2.  Give the principal parts for the verb from which *crevit* (line 60) is formed. Provide the meaning for each part.

    a.  *cresco*                           **I grow, I increase**

    b.  *crescere*                         **to grow, to increase**

    c.  *crevi*                            **I have grown, I have increased, I grew**

    d.  *cretum*                           **having been increased**

3.  Give the nominative and genitive singular, gender, and meaning for *iure* (line 60).

    **ius, iuris (n.) authority, jurisdiction, power, right**

4.  Give the principal parts and meaning for the verb from which *loquuntur* (line 63) is formed.

    a.  *loquor*                           **I speak**

    b.  *loqui*                            **to speak**

    c.  *locutus sum*                      **I have spoken**

5.  Give the positive and superlative forms and meanings for *magis* (line 64).

    a.  *magnopere*                        **greatly**

    b.  *maxime*                           **especially, very, in the highest degree**

6.  Give the nominative singular forms for *utrique* (line 66). Give the English for this pronoun.

    a.  *uterque, utraque, utrumque*

    b.  **each, each of two**

7.  Give the genitive, gender, and meaning for *paries* (line 66).

    **paries, parietis (m.) wall**

8.  Give the principal parts and meanings for the verb *constiterant* (line 71).

    a.  *consto*                           **I take up a position, I stand with**

    b.  *constare*                         **to take up a position, to stand with**

    c.  *constiti*                         **I have taken up a position, I stood with**

9. Give the nominative singular form and meaning for *amantibus* (line 73).

   ***amans*—loving**

10. a. Write out the four principal parts of the verb *eo*.

   ***eo, ire, ii (ivi), itum (iturus)***

   b. Find all the compounds of *eo* in the *Pyramus and Thisbe* episode. Give the Latin verb form and meaning for each and provide line references in parentheses for your Latin choices.

   1. *coissent*—**they would have joined together, they would have united (line 60)**

   2. *coiere*— **they joined (alternative form of third person plural *coierunt*) (line 83)**

   3. *exierint*—**they would go out (line 86)**

   4. *exit*—**goes out, departs (line 92)**

   5. *redit*—**it returns (line 103)**

   6. *redit*—**she returns (line 129)**

# DAEDALUS AND ICARUS
# METAMORPHOSES 8.183–235

     Daedalus interea Creten longumque perosus
     exilium tactusque loci natalis amore
185    clausus erat pelago. "terras licet" inquit "et undas
     obstruat: et caelum certe patet; ibimus illac:
     omnia possideat, non possidet aera Minos."
     dixit et ignotas animum dimittit in artes
     naturamque novat. nam ponit in ordine pennas
190    a minima coeptas, longam breviore sequenti,
     ut clivo crevisse putes: sic rustica quondam
     fistula disparibus paulatim surgit avenis;
     tum lino medias et ceris alligat imas
     atque ita conpositas parvo curvamine flectit,
195    ut veras imitetur aves. puer Icarus una
     stabat et, ignarus sua se tractare pericla,
     ore renidenti modo, quas vaga moverat aura,
     captabat plumas, flavam modo pollice ceram
     mollibat lusuque suo mirabile patris
200    impediebat opus. postquam manus ultima coepto
     inposita est, geminas opifex libravit in alas
     ipse suum corpus motaque pependit in aura;
     instruit et natum "medio" que "ut limite curras,
     Icare," ait "moneo, ne, si demissior ibis,
205    unda gravet pennas, si celsior, ignis adurat:
     inter utrumque vola. nec te spectare Booten
     aut Helicen iubeo strictumque Orionis ensem:
     me duce carpe viam!" pariter praecepta volandi
     tradit et ignotas umeris accommodat alas.
210    inter opus monitusque genae maduere seniles,
     et patriae tremuere manus; dedit oscula nato
     non iterum repetenda suo pennisque levatus
     ante volat comitique timet, velut ales, ab alto
     quae teneram prolem produxit in aera nido,
215    hortaturque sequi damnosasque erudit artes
     et movet ipse suas et nati respicit alas.
     hos aliquis tremula dum captat harundine pisces,
     aut pastor baculo stivave innixus arator
     vidit et obstipuit, quique aethera carpere possent,
220    credidit esse deos. et iam Iunonia laeva

parte Samos (fuerant Delosque Parosque relictae)
dextra Lebinthos erat fecundaque melle Calymne,
cum puer audaci coepit gaudere volatu
deseruitque ducem caelique cupidine tractus
225    altius egit iter. rapidi vicinia solis
mollit odoratas, pennarum vincula, ceras;
tabuerant cerae: nudos quatit ille lacertos,
remigioque carens non ullas percipit auras,
oraque caerulea patrium clamantia nomen
230    excipiuntur aqua, quae nomen traxit ab illo.
at pater infelix, nec iam pater, "Icare," dixit,
"Icare," dixit "ubi es? qua te regione requiram?"
"Icare," dicebat: pennas adspexit in undis
devovitque suas artes corpusque sepulcro
235    condidit, et tellus a nomine dicta sepulti.

# Short Answer Questions

Line 185    What is the case and use of *pelago*? **ablative of means**

Line 190    What is the form of *coeptas*? **perfect passive participle (of *coepi*)**

What word does it modify? ***pennas* (line 189)**

Translate *coeptas*. **"beginning (having begun)"**

What form of the verb is *sequenti*? **present active participle**

What are the principal parts of this verb? ***sequor, sequi, secutus sum***

Translate *breviore sequenti*. **"with the shorter following"**

What is the case and use of *breviore sequenti*? **ablative absolute**

Line 191    What is the form of *putes*? **second person singular present subjunctive active**

How is this form used? **result/consecutive clause**

Line 194    What is the case and use of *curvamine*? **ablative of manner**

Line 196    What is the reason for the form *tractare*? **infinitive in indirect statement**

What is the subject of *tractare*? ***se***

Line 199    What case is *mirabile*? **accusative**

What word does *mirabile* modify? ***opus* (line 200)**

Line 203      What is the form of *curras?* **second person singular present subjunctive active**

                   How is this form used? **indirect command (after *moneo,* line 204)**

Line 206      What is the form of *spectare?* **present active infinitive**

                   How is this form used? **with *iubeo* (line 207)/accusative with infinitive following *iubeo* expressing command**

Line 209      What is the case and use of *umeris?* **dative with compound verb (*accommodat*)**

Line 211      What is the case and use of *nato?* **dative, indirect object of *dedit***

Line 212      What is the form of *repetenda?* **future passive participle (gerundive)**

                   What word does *repetenda* modify? ***oscula* (line 211)**

                   Translate *repetenda.* **"to be repeated/about to be repeated/going to be repeated"**

Line 218      What is the case and use of *baculo?* **dative with compound verb (*innixus*)**

Line 224      What is the form of *tractus?* **perfect passive participle (of *traho*)**

                   What word does *tractus* modify? ***puer* (line 223)**

Line 229      What is the form of *clamantia?* **present active participle**

                   What is the number and case of *clamantia?* **nominative plural**

                   What word does *clamantia* modify? ***ora***

# Multiple Choice Questions *Suggested time: 12 minutes*

1.   The metrical pattern for the first four feet of line 183 is
     a.  dactyl-spondee-dactyl-spondee      **b.  dactyl-dactyl-spondee-spondee**
     c.  spondee-dactyl-spondee-dactyl      d.  spondee-dactyl-dactyl-spondee

2.   Line 187 (*omnia . . . Minos*) is best translated as
     a.  he possesses omens, Minos does not possess the air      **b.  let Minos possess all things, he does not possess the air**
     c.  all things possess Minos, the air does not possess Minos      d.  let all things own Minos, he does not own the air

3.   Line 189 contains which figure of speech?
     a.  onomatopoeia      b.  asyndeton
     **c.  alliteration**      d.  hyperbole

4.  In line 208, *me duce* is an
    a.  ablative of personal agent
    **c.  ablative absolute**
    b.  ablative of manner
    d.  ablative of separation

5.  The figure of speech expressed by *movet ipse suas* (line 216) is
    a.  irony
    **c.  ellipsis**
    b.  hyperbole
    d.  hendiadys

6.  In lines 217–220, the observers believe that Daedalus and Icarus are gods because
    a   they are afraid
    **c.  they can fly**
    b.  they are amazed
    d.  they can seize the air

7.  The antecedent of *quae* (line 230) is
    a.  *ora* (line 229)
    **c.  *aqua* (line 230)**
    b.  *nomen* (line 230)
    d.  *caerulea* (line 229)

8.  Lines 229–230 contain both a double chiasmus and interlocked word order (synchesis). The effect of these figures is
    a.  division between father and son
    **c.  a mirroring of Icarus' fateful spiraling fall**
    b.  the depiction of the love between father and son
    d.  creation of an image of sea waves

9.  What use of the ablative is *sepulcro* (line 234)?
    a.  means
    **c.  place where**
    b.  manner
    d.  agent

10. In lines 229 and 235, the poet provides two examples of *aitia* based on the name of
    a.  Daedalus
    c.  an island
    b.  the ocean
    **d.  Icarus**

# Translation *Suggested time: 15 minutes*

Translate the passage below as literally as possible.

> dixit et ignotas animum dimittit in artes
> naturamque novat. nam ponit in ordine pennas
> a minima coeptas, longam breviore sequenti,
> ut clivo crevisse putes: sic rustica quondam
> 5      fistula disparibus paulatim surgit avenis;
> tum lino medias et ceris alligat imas
> atque ita conpositas parvo curvamine flectit,
> ut veras imitetur aves.

*Metamorphoses 8.188–195*

He spoke and directs his mind to unknown arts and makes nature new. For he puts feathers in order, beginning from the smallest, the shorter following the long, so that you would think they had grown on a slope: thus once the rural panpipe rises little by little with unequal reeds; then he fastens the middle [feathers] with thread and the lowest ones with wax and bends them placed together thus in a small curve so that he imitates a real bird.

**18 chunks. 9 points total, 1/2 point each. Round up to nearest whole point.**

| | |
|---|---|
| *dixit* | **he spoke** |
| *et ... animum dimittit* | **and he directs/sends his mind** |
| *ignotas ... in artes* | **into unknown arts** |
| *naturamque novat* | **and he makes nature new** |
| *nam ponit in ordine* | **for he puts in order** |
| *pennas coeptas* | **feathers beginning** |
| *a minima* | **from the smallest** |
| *longam breviore sequenti* | **the shorter following the long** |
| *ut clivo crevisse putes* | **so that you would think they had grown on a slant/slope** |
| *sic rustica quondam fistula* | **thus the rustic/rural panpipe once/formerly** |
| *paulatim surgit* | **rises little by little** |
| *disparibus avenis* | **with unequal reeds** |
| *tum lino medias ... alligat* | **then with thread he binds together the middle (feathers)** |
| *et ceris ... imas* | **and with wax the lowest (feathers)** |
| *atque ita conpositas ... flectit* | **and he bends the placed together (feathers) thus/in such a way** |
| *parvo curvamine* | **in a small curve** |
| *ut ... imitetur* | **so that he imitates** |
| *versas ... aves* | **real birds** |

# Short Analysis Questions

1. List two ways in which Icarus hinders his father's work (lines 195–200). Be sure to use Latin words in your answer.

   a. **He catches the feathers that move in the breeze—*captabat plumas qua vaga moverat.***

   b. **He softens the wax with his thumb—*flavam modo police ceram.***

   c. What is Icarus's state of mind in this passage? Again, use Latin words as examples in your response.

      **He is ignorant (*ignarus*) of the dangers he will face; he stands near with face beaming, (*ore renidenti*).**

2. What four instructions does Daedalus give to Icarus? Use Latin words in your response.

   a. **Not to fly too low (*demissior*) so that his wings will not get wet (*ne unda gravet pennas*).**

   b. **Not to fly too high (*celsior*) so that fire burns him (*ignis adurat*).**

   c. **Fly in the middle (*inter utrumque vola*).**

   d. **Not to look at the constellations (*nec te spectare Booten aut Helicen strictumque Orionis ensem*).**

3. Why does the poet call the wings *ignotas* in line 209?

   **Because no one has ever made wings and flown with them before. The skill is unknown.**

4. a. Translate *velut ales, ab alto/ quae teneram prolem produxit in aera nido,/ hortaturque sequi* (lines 213–215).

      **Just as a bird, which has led its young offspring from the high nest into the air, and he urges him to follow.**

   b. Briefly explain the appropriateness of this simile.

      **The simile is very apt because like the bird, Daedalus is teaching his son how to fly.**

## Essay *Suggested time: 20 minutes*

The story of Daedalus and Icarus illustrates the ancient maxim, "nothing in excess," carved on the temple of Apollo at Delphi. Write an essay in which you discuss how the actions of both father and son are illustrative of the importance of this maxim.

Support your assertions with references drawn from **throughout** the passage. All Latin words must be copied or their line numbers provided, AND they must be translated or paraphrased closely enough so that it is clear you understand the Latin. It is your responsibility to convince your reader that you are basing your conclusions on the Latin text and not merely on a general recollection of the passage. Direct your answer to the question; do not merely summarize the passage. Please write your essay on a separate piece of paper.

**The question asks the students to argue that the story of Daedalus and Icarus illustrates the dangers of going beyond what is appropriate or natural. At the same time, the poet suggests that the flight of Daedalus and Icarus was heroic in that it was an attempt to flee imprisonment through the creation of wings for human flight. Students should construct an argument that shows the ambiguity of the temple's famous maxim. Among the lines that might be chosen to illustrate this argument are (lines 188–9; 199–200; 209; 203–9; 215; 218–220; 223; 234–5).**

**6 – A fully developed essay that presents an argument that shows that the student understands the ambivalence of the speaker about the temple's maxim. Latin examples are well chosen and correctly cited.**

**5 – A strong essay with a good analysis of the complexity of the passage, but one whose arguments are not fully developed. Latin is correctly cited.**

**4 – A competent analytical response, but one that that does not reveal an understanding of the duality of the passage. Latin examples are weak.**

**3 – A less competent response that is too descriptive and uses insufficient or inappropriate or no Latin examples.**

**2 – An essay that is vague, general, and non-analytical. The cited Latin demonstrates that the student has a poor understanding of the passage.**

**1 – An incoherent response, although it may contain some pertinent points.**

**0 – The response is irrelevant to the topic or incorrect, or merely restates the question without any analysis.**

# Scansion

Scan the following lines.

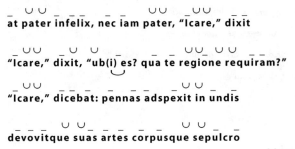

_Metamorphoses 8.231–234_

# Vocabulary

1.  List all the nouns for birds, feathers, and flight. Provide the dictionary entry and the meaning for each word. Provide line references in parentheses beside each Latin word you list.

    a.  *pennas* (line 189) *penna, -ae* (f.) feather

    b.  *aves* (line 195) *avis, -is* (f.) bird

    c.  *plumas* (line 198) *pluma, -ae* (f.) feather

    d.  *alas* (line 201) *ala, -ae* (f.) wing

    e.  *ales* (line 213) *ales, alitis,* (f.) bird

    f.  *nido* (line 214) *nidus, -i* (m.) nest

    g.  *alas* (see d.)

    h.  *volatu* (line 223) *volatus, -us* (m.) flying, flight

    i.  *remigio,* (line 228) *remigium, -i* (n.) oars, wings

2.  List all the principal parts and meaning for all verbs that refer to movement of the body or to flight. Provide line references in parentheses beside each Latin word you list.

    a.  *ibimus* **(line 186)** *eo, ire, ivi (ii), itum (iturum) go*

    b.  *moverat* **(line 197)** *moveo, -ere, movi, motum* **move**

    c.  *pependit* **(line 202)** *pendeo, -ere, pependi* **hang**

    d.  *curras* **(line 203)** *curo, currere, cucurri, cursum* **to run, fly quickly**

    e.  *vola* **(line 206)** *volo, -are, -avi, -atum* **fly**

    f.  *volandi* **(line 208) see e.**

    g.  *levatus* **(line 212)** *levo, -are, -avi, -atum* **lift**

    h.  *volat* **(line 213) see e.**

    i.  *movet* **(line 216) see b.**

    j.  *innixus* **(line 218)** *innitor, -i, nixus* **– lean on**

    k.  *egit iter* **(line 225)** *ago, agere, egi, actum* **do, drive—here to fly**

    l.  *quatit* **(line 227)** *quatio, quatere, quassum* **shake**

# PHILEMON AND BAUCIS
# METAMORPHOSES 8.616–650

obstipuere omnes nec talia dicta probarunt,
ante omnesque Lelex animo maturus et aevo,
sic ait: "inmensa est finemque potentia caeli
non habet, et quicquid superi voluere, peractum est,
620    quoque minus dubites, tiliae contermina quercus
collibus est Phrygiis modico circumdata muro;
ipse locum vidi; nam me Pelopeia Pittheus
misit in arva suo quondam regnata parenti.
haud procul hinc stagnum est, tellus habitabilis olim,
625    nunc celebres mergis fulicisque palustribus undae;
Iuppiter huc specie mortali cumque parente
venit Atlantiades positis caducifer alis.
mille domos adiere locum requiemque petentes,
mille domos clausere serae; tamen una recepit,
630    parva quidem, stipulis et canna tecta palustri,
sed pia Baucis anus parilique aetate Philemon
illa sunt annis iuncti iuvenalibus, illa
consenuere casa paupertatemque fatendo
effecere levem nec iniqua mente ferendo;
635    nec refert, dominos illic famulosne requiras:
tota domus duo sunt, idem parentque iubentque.
ergo ubi caelicolae parvos tetigere penates
summissoque humiles intrarunt vertice postes,
membra senex posito iussit relevare sedili;
640    cui superiniecit textum rude sedula Baucis
inque foco tepidum cinerem dimovit et ignes
suscitat hesternos foliisque et cortice sicco
nutrit et ad flammas anima producit anili
multifidasque faces ramaliaque arida tecto
645    detulit et minuit parvoque admovit aeno,
quodque suus coniunx riguo conlegerat horto,
truncat holus foliis; furca levat ille bicorni
sordida terga suis nigro pendentia tigno
servatoque diu resecat de tergore partem
650    exiguam sectamque domat ferventibus undis.

## Short Answer Questions

Line 616      What is the form of *obstipuere*? **third person plural perfect indicative active (alternate for *obstipuerunt*)**

Line 617      What is the case and use of the two words *animo . . . aevo*? **ablative of specification/ respect**

Lines 618–619      What subject do *est* (618) and *habet* (619) share? **potentia caeli (line 618)**

Line 619      With which word does *peractum* agree? **quicquid**

Line 620      What two words agree with *quercus*? **contermina (line 620) and circumdata (line 621)**

Line 625      What word does *celebres* modify? **undae**

Line 628      What is the subject of *adiere*? **petentes**

Line 629      What is the subject of *clausere*? **serae**

     What noun does *una* modify? **an understood *domus***

Line 631      What type of ablative is *parilique aetate*? **ablative of description**

Line 634      What noun does *levem* modify? **paupertatem (line 633)**

Line 639      What is the missing subject for *relevare*? **supply, as missing, "*eos*" referring to the gods**

Lines 641–647      What is the subject for *dimovit* (line 641), *suscitat* (line 642), *nutrit* (line 643), *producit* (line 643), *detulit* (line 645), *minuit* (line 645), *admovit* (line 645), and *truncat* (line 647)? **sedula Baucis (line 640)**

Line 647      What is the subject of *levat*? **ille (Philemon)**

## Multiple Choice Questions *Suggested time: 12 minutes*

1. According to Lelex, in lines 618–619,
   a. he does not believe the gods are all powerful
   **b. the gods are all powerful**
   c. the gods do not have great power
   d. the gods do not dwell in heaven

2. The best translation for *tiliae contermina quercus* (line 620) is
   a. a linden tree's oak nearby
   **b. an oak adjacent to a linden tree**
   c. an oak and a linden tree nearby
   d. a linden tree adjacent to an oak

3. Which of the following figures of speech can be found in line 625 (*nunc . . . undae*)?
   a. hyperbaton
   b. alliteration
   **c. chiasmus**
   d. synchesis

4. To whom is *Atlantiades* (line 627) a reference?

   a. Atlas
   b. Jupiter
   **c. Mercury**
   d. Atalanta

5. The best translation for the phrase *mille domos clausere serae* (line 629) is

   a. a thousand homes closed their crossbars
   **b. a thousand crossbars closed their homes**
   c. the houses closed a thousand crossbars
   d. crossbars closed the homes a thousand times

6. What is the case and number of both *illa* and *illa* in line 632?

   a. nominative singular
   **b. ablative singular**
   c. nominative plural
   d. accusative plural

7. The best translation for *paupertatemque . . . ferendo* (lines 633–34) is

   a. they made their poverty light and not resentful by professing it and bearing it
   b. they bore their poverty with a not resentful mind and made it light by professing it
   c. they professed their poverty and bore it with a not resentful mind making it light
   **d. by professing their poverty and by bearing it with a not resentful mind they made it light**

8. The metrical pattern of the first four feet of line 644 is

   a. dactyl-dactyl-dactyl-dactyl
   b. dactyl-dactyl-spondee-spondee
   c. dactyl-spondee-dactyl-dactyl
   **d. dactyl-dactyl-spondee-dactyl**

9. Lines 646–647 contain an example of

   a. assonance
   b. a golden line
   c. synchesis
   **d. prolepsis**

10. In lines 647–650, we learn that

    a the vegetables are prepared
    b the couch is prepared
    **c. the meat is prepared**
    d. the fire is prepared

## Translation *Suggested time: 15 minutes*

Translate the passage below as literally as possible.

> "inmensa est finemque potentia caeli
> non habet, et quicquid superi voluere, peractum est,
> quoque minus dubites, tiliae contermina quercus
> collibus est Phrygiis modico circumdata muro;
> 5     ipse locum vidi; nam me Pelopeia Pittheus
> misit in arva suo quondam regnata parenti.
>
> *Metamorphoses 8.618–623*

"The power of heaven is mighty and has no end, and whatever the gods have desired, has been carried out. And, so that you may be less doubtful, [know that] there is an oak tree near by a linden on the Phrygian hills, surrounded by a modest wall; I myself have seen the place; for Pittheus sent me to the territory of Pelops formerly ruled by his father.

**18 chunks. 9 points total, ½ point each. Round up to nearest whole point.**

| | |
|---|---|
| *potentia caeli* | **the power of the heavens/heaven** |
| *immensa est* | **is immense/mighty** |
| *finemque* | **and no end** |
| *non habet* | **does it have** |
| *et quicquid* | **and whatever** |
| *superi voluere* | **the gods above have desired** |
| *peractum est* | **has been carried out** |
| *quoque minus dubites* | **and so that you may doubt less/be less doubtful** |
| *tiliae contermina quercus* | **an oak tree next to a linden tree** |
| *collibus est Phrygiis* | **there is in/on the Phrygian hills** |
| *circumdata* | **surrounded** |
| *modico . . . muro* | **by a modest wall** |
| *ipse locum vidi* | **I myself have seen the place** |
| *nam me . . . Pittheus misit* | **for Pittheus sent me** |
| *Pelopeia . . . in arva* | **into the Pelopeian fields/territory** |
| *quondam* | **once/formerly** |
| *regnata* | **governed/ruled** |
| *suo . . . parenti* | **by his father** |

## Short Analysis Questions

1.   How does the embracing word order of line 621, *modico circumdata muro*, reinforce the meaning of the phrase?

      **Because *circumdata* modifies the *quercus*, then the words *modico . . . muro* surround *contermina* just as the wall surrounds the oak tree.**

2. Line 637 (*ergo . . . penates*) contains a metonymy. Write out the Latin that expresses the metonymy and explain why it qualifies as a metonymy.

**Penates is used metonymously because although it literally refers to the household gods, here it refers to the structure of the house.**

3. In lines 641–645 (*inque . . . detulit*), we are given a **very** detailed account of how Baucis prepares the fire. Write out three Latin noun and adjective phrases that describe the materials Baucis used in her preparation. Translate each of your choices.

**tepidum cinerem—warm ashes**

**hesternos ignes—yesterday's fire**

**cortice sicco—dry bark**

**multifidas faces—split firebrands**

**ramalia arida—dry twigs**

# Vocabulary

Below you will find a list of high-frequency words you have encountered in your recent readings. For all the words you know, write out full dictionary entries, including English meanings, and put a √ mark in the left-hand column to show you have already committed these words to memory. For any words you do not yet know, write out the dictionary entries using the end glossary and learn them as soon as possible.

√

1. ____ *aiō* _____

2. ____ *āla* _____

3. ____ *amans* _____

4. ____ *aqua* _____

5. ____ *caelum* _____

6. ____ *captō* _____

7. ____ *cingō* _____

8. ____ *coniunx* _____

9. ____ *corpus* _____

10. ____ *crescō* _____

11. ____ *cum* preposition _____

12. ____ *cum* conjunction _____

13. ____ *custōs* _____

14. ____ *domus* _____

15. ____ *dum* _____

16. ____ *duo* _____

17. ____ *fallō* _____

18. ____ *ferō* _____

19. ____ *fīō* _____

20. ____ *foris* _____

21. ____ *ignis* _____

22. ____ *iubeō* _____

23. ____ *iuvenis* _____

24. ____ *locus* _____

25. ____ *loquor* _____

26. ____ *nē* _____

27. ____ *pars* _____

28. ____ *parvus* _____

29. ____ *pōnō* _____

30. ____ *tellus* _____

31. ____ *ubi* _____

32. ____ *unda* _____

# PHILEMON AND BAUCIS
# METAMORPHOSES 8.651–678

651*  interea medias fallunt sermonibus horas
655   concutiuntque torum de molli fluminis ulva
      inpositum lecto sponda pedibusque salignis.
      vestibus hunc velant, quas non nisi tempore festo
      sternere consuerant, sed et haec vilisque vetusque
      vestis erat, lecto non indignanda saligno.
660   adcubuere dei. mensam succincta tremensque
      ponit anus, mensae sed erat pes tertius inpar:
      testa parem fecit; quae postquam subdita clivum
      sustulit, aequatam mentae tersere virentes.
      ponitur hic bicolor sincerae baca Minervae
665   conditaque in liquida corna autumnalia faece
      intibaque et radix et lactis massa coacti
      ovaque non acri leviter versata favilla,
      omnia fictilibus. post haec caelatus eodem
      sistitur argento crater fabricataque fago
670   pocula, qua cava sunt, flaventibus inlita ceris;
      parva mora est, epulasque foci misere calentes,
      nec longae rursus referuntur vina senectae
      dantque locum mensis paulum seducta secundis:
      hic nux, hic mixta est rugosis carica palmis
675   prunaque et in patulis redolentia mala canistris
      et de purpureis conlectae vitibus uvae,
      candidus in medio favus est; super omnia vultus
      accessere boni nec iners pauperque voluntas.

## Short Answer Questions

Line 657   What is the antecedent of *quas*? **vestibus**

Line 660   What is the form of *adcubuere*? **third person plural perfect indicative active
           (alternate for *adcubuerunt*)**

           Which noun does *succinta* modify? **anus (line 661)**

Line 661   On which noun is the genitive *mensae* dependent? **pes**

Line 663   What is the subject of *tersere*? **mentae ... virentes**

---

*   Four lines, 652–655a, are of questionable authenticity and are omitted from this text.

Line 664      What are all the subjects of *ponitur*? Provide line references in parentheses for your Latin choices. **bicolor baca (line 664), *corna autumnalia* (line 665), *intiba* ( line 666), *radix* (line 666), *massa* (line 666), *ova* (line 667)**

Line 668      What word does *caelatus* modify? **crater (line 669)**

Line 678      What are all the subjects of *accessere*? **vultus... *boni* (lines 677–678), *iners pauperque voluntas* (line 678)**

## Multiple Choice Questions *Suggested time: 10 minutes*

1. With what noun does *indignanda* (line 659) agree?
   a. *anus* (line 661)       **b. *vestis* (line 659)**
   c. *sponda* (line 656)       d. *mensam* (line 660)

2. *non indignanda* (line 659) is an example of
   a. chiasmus       b. irony
   c. alliteration       **d. litotes**

3. What is the antecedent of *quae* (line 662)?
   **a. *testa* (line 662)**       b. *pes* (line 661)
   c. *clivum* (line 662)       d. *mensae* (line 661)

4. The best translation for line 667 (*ovaque . . . favilla*) is
   a. eggs turned lightly not in warm ashes       **b. eggs turned lightly in warm ashes**
   c. not eggs turned lightly in warm ashes       d. eggs not turned lightly in warm ashes

5. From line 672 (*nec longae . . . senectae*), we learn that
   a. well-aged wines are drunk       b. the old man and woman bring out country wines
   **c. young wine is drunk throughout the meal**       d. no wine is drunk during the meal

6. The best translation for line 674 (*hic . . . palmis*) is
   a. here a nut, here wrinkly date mixed with figs       b. this nut, this fig mixed with wrinkly date
   **c. here a nut, here a fig mixed with wrinkly dates**       d. this nut, this date mixed with wrinkly fig

7. From lines 677–678 (*super . . . voluntas*), we learn that

   **a. happy faces and good will abounded**
   b. the faces of good people and good will abounded
   c. the faces of happy people and lazy spirits were present
   d. it is clear the guests would rather not be present

8. The metrical pattern for the first four feet of line 678 is

   a. dactyl-dactyl-spondee-spondee
   b. dactyl-spondee-spondee-dactyl
   c. dactyl-spondee-dactyl-spondee
   **d. spondee-dactyl-dactyl-spondee**

## Translation *Suggested time: 15 minutes*

Translate the passage below as literally as possible.

> vestibus hunc velant, quas non nisi tempore festo
> sternere consuerant, sed et haec vilisque vetusque
> vestis erat, lecto non indignanda saligno.
> adcubuere dei. mensam succincta tremensque
> 5   ponit anus, mensae sed erat pes tertius inpar:
> testa parem fecit; quae postquam subdita clivum
> sustulit, aequatam mentae tersere virentes.

Metamorphoses 8.657–663

**They covered this with cloths, which they had not been accustomed to use except on festive days, but even this cloth was common and old, not unsuitable for a willow couch. The gods reclined at table. The old woman, with her skirt bound up and trembling, sets up the table, but the third foot was uneven, she made it straight with a piece of earthenware; which, after placed beneath held up the slope, green mint wiped off the leveled table.**

**18 chunks. 9 points total, ½ point each. Round up to nearest whole point.**

| | |
|---|---|
| *vestibus hunc velant* | **this they cover with cloths** |
| *quas* | **which** |
| *non . . . sternere consuerant* | **they had not been accustomed to spread out** |
| *nisi tempore festo* | **unless/except on festive days/a time of festival** |
| *sed et haec . . . vestis erat* | **but even this cloth was** |
| *vilisque vetusque* | **common/ordinary and old** |
| *non indignanda* | **not unworthy** |
| *lecto . . . saligno* | **of the willow couch** |
| *adcubuere dei* | **the gods reclined** |
| *succinta tremensque* | **with her skirt bound up and trembling** |
| *mensam . . . ponit anus* | **the old woman sets up the table** |

| | |
|---|---|
| *mensae sed ... pes tertius* | **but the third foot of the table** |
| *erat ... inpar* | **was uneven** |
| *testa parem fecit* | **a shard made it level** |
| *quae postquam subdita* | **which after it had been put underneath** |
| *clivum sustulit* | **held up the incline** |
| *mentae ... virentes* | **green/fresh mint** |
| *aequatam ... tersere* | **wiped clean the leveled (table)** |

# Short Analysis Questions

1. Write out the Latin and explain a polysyndeton and alliteration from the phrase *sed et haec vilisque vetusque / vestis erat* (lines 658–659).

   **vilisque vetusque—polysyndeton (double *que*)**

   **vilisque vetusque vestis—alliteration ("v" sounds)**

   **Both these figures of speech draw attention to the humble and worn appearance of the cloth, reinforcing the poverty of Philemon and Baucis.**

2. a. Write out the Latin that expresses a chiasmus in line 665.

   **A       B       B       A**
   **liquida corna autumnalia faece**

   b. Explain how this chiasmus reinforces the meaning of the line.

   **The autumnal cornelian cherries literally sit inside the liquid that preserves them.**

3. Explain the transferred epithet in line 676 (*et de purpureis ... uvae*).

   **Purpureis grammatically modifies vitibus (the vines) when in fact it is the uvae (grapes) that are purple.**

# Vocabulary

Below you will find a list of high-frequency words you have encountered in your recent readings. For all the words you know, write out full dictionary entries, including English meanings, and put a √ mark in the left-hand column to show you have already committed these words to memory. For any words you do not yet know, write out the dictionary entries using the end glossary and learn them as soon as possible.

√

1. _____ *āēr* _____

2. _____ *altus* _____

3. _____ *animus* _____

4. _____ *caedēs* _____

5. _____ *cera* _____

6. _____ *cognoscō* _____

7. _____ *mollis* _____

8. _____ *mora* _____

9. _____ *mensa* _____

10. _____ *pōmum* _____

11. _____ *postquam* _____

12. _____ *relinquō* _____

13. _____ *sanguinis* _____

14. _____ *sentiō* _____

15. _____ *signum* _____

16. _____ *tangō* _____

17. _____ *tenuis* _____

18. _____ *timidus* _____

19. _____ *tingō* _____

20. _____ *transeō* _____

21. _____ *umbra* _____

22. ____ *tegō* _____

23. ____ *veniō* _____

24. ____ *verbum* _____

25. ____ *vestigium* _____

26. ____ *vestis* _____

27. ____ *vetō* _____

28. ____ *volō* _____

29. ____ *votum* _____

30. ____ *vultus* _____

# PHILEMON AND BAUCIS
# METAMORPHOSES 8.679–724

"Interea totiens haustum cratera repleri
680 sponte sua per seque vident succrescere vina:
attoniti novitate pavent manibusque supinis
concipiunt Baucisque preces timidusque Philemon
et veniam dapibus nullisque paratibus orant.
unicus anser erat, minimae custodia villae:
685 quem dis hospitibus domini mactare parabant;
ille celer penna tardos aetate fatigat
eluditque diu tandemque est visus ad ipsos
confugisse deos: superi vetuere necari
'di' que 'sumus, meritasque luet vicinia poenas
690 inpia' dixerunt; 'vobis inmunibus huius
esse mali dabitur; modo vestra relinquite tecta
ac nostros comitate gradus et in ardua montis
ite simul!' parent ambo baculisque levati
nituntur longo vestigia ponere clivo.
695 tantum aberant summo, quantum semel ire sagitta
missa potest: flexere oculos et mersa palude
cetera prospiciunt, tantum sua tecta manere,
dumque ea mirantur, dum deflent fata suorum,
illa vetus, dominis etiam casa parva duobus
700 vertitur in templum: furcas subiere columnae,
stramina flavescunt aurataque tecta videntur
caelataeque fores adopertaque marmore tellus.
talia tum placido Saturnius edidit ore:
'dicite, iuste senex et femina coniuge iusto
705 digna, quid optetis.' cum Baucide pauca locutus
iudicium superis aperit commune Philemon:
'esse sacerdotes delubraque vestra tueri
poscimus, et quoniam concordes egimus annos,
auferat hora duos eadem, nec coniugis umquam
710 busta meae videam, neu sim tumulandus ab illa.'
vota fides sequitur: templi tutela fuere,
donec vita data est; annis aevoque soluti
ante gradus sacros cum starent forte locique
narrarent casus, frondere Philemona Baucis,
715 Baucida conspexit senior frondere Philemon.

iamque super geminos crescente cacumine vultus
mutua, dum licuit, reddebant dicta 'vale' que
'o coniunx' dixere simul, simul abdita texit
ora frutex: ostendit adhuc Thyneius illic
720    incola de gemino vicinos corpore truncos.
haec mihi non vani (neque erat, cur fallere vellent)
narravere senes; equidem pendentia vidi
serta super ramos ponensque recentia dixi
'cura deum di sint, et, qui coluere, colantur.'"

# Short Answer Questions

Line 679    Which noun does *haustum* modify? **cratera**

Line 681    What case is *attoniti?* **nominative**

With what does it agree? ***Baucis* (line 682) and *Philemon* (line 682)**

Line 683    What is the case and use of *dapibus nullisque paratibus?* **ablative of specification**

Lines 692–693    Of what verb form are *comitate* (line 692) and *ite* (line 693) examples? **second person plural present imperative active**

Line 693    What is the case and use of *baculis?* **ablative of means**

On which other word in this line does it depend? ***levati***

Line 696    What is the form of *flexere?* **third person plural perfect indicative active (alternate of flexerunt)**

Line 704    What case are *senex* and *femina?* **vocative**

Line 705    What verb form is *locutus?* **perfect passive participle (*loquor*, deponent)**

What are the principal parts of the verb from which *locutus* is formed? ***loquor, loqui, locutus sum***

Which noun does *locutus* modify? ***Philemon* (line 706)**

Lines 709–710    What three jussive subjunctive verbs form their request in these lines? ***auferat, videam, sim tumulandus***

Line 712    With which words does the participle *soluti* agree? ***Baucis* (line 714) and *Philemon* (line 715)**

Line 714    What is the subject of *frondere?* ***Philemona***

## Multiple Choice Questions *Suggested time: 12 minutes*

1. To whom does *superi* (line 688) refer?

   a. Philemon and Baucis

   **b. Jupiter and Mercury**

   c. the gods of Olympus

   d. the old people

2. What is the case and number of *gradus* (line 692)?

   a. nominative plural

   b. nominative singular

   c. genitive singular

   **d. accusative plural**

3. From lines 695–696, we learn that

   **a. Philemon and Baucis have nearly reached the top of the mountain**

   b. Philemon and Baucis have a long way to go to reach the top of the mountain

   c. Philemon and Baucis flee because they are being shot at with arrows

   d. Philemon and Baucis begin to shoot arrows at their neighbors

4. In line 703, *Saturnius* refers to

   a. Saturn

   b. Mercury

   **c. Jupiter**

   d. the temple

5. The best translation for lines 704–705 (*dicite . . . digna*) is

   a. tell the just man and the woman's just husband

   b. tell, just old man, worthy of a just female wife

   **c. tell, just old man and woman worthy of a just husband**

   d. old man, tell your wife, worthy of a just husband

6. The best translation for line 716 (*iamque . . . vultus*) is

   **a. and now with a treetop growing over their twin faces**

   b. and now a treetop grows over their twin faces

   c. and now over their twin faces grows a treetop

   d. and now twin treetops grow over their faces

7. The metrical pattern of the first four feet of line 720 is

   a. dactyl-spondee-dactyl-spondee

   b. dactyl-dactyl-dactyl-spondee

   c. dactyl-spondee-spondee-spondee

   **d. dactyl-dactyl-spondee-spondee**

8. The figure of speech found in line 720 is

   a. synecdoche

   **b. synchesis**

   c. chiasmus

   d. hyperbaton

9. Who is the subject of *vidi* (line 722)?

   a. Philemon                 **b. Lelex**

   c. Baucis                   d. Thyneius

10. The best translation for *cura deum di sint* (line 724) is

   a. let the gods care for those who are gods      **b. let those who are a care of the gods be gods**

   c. let the gods worship those who are a care to the gods      d. let those whom the gods worship be gods

## Translation *Suggested time: 15 minutes*

Translate the passage below as literally as possible.

> tantum aberant summo, quantum semel ire sagitta
> missa potest: flexere oculos et mersa palude
> cetera prospiciunt, tantum sua tecta manere,
> dumque ea mirantur, dum deflent fata suorum,
> 5   illa vetus, dominis etiam casa parva duobus
> vertitur in templum: furcas subiere columnae,
> stramina flavescunt aurataque tecta videntur
> caelataeque fores adopertaque marmore tellus.
>
>                    *Metamorphoses 8.695–702*

**They were only as far from the top as an arrow once shot can go; they turned their eyes and see the rest flooded by a swamp; only their own house remains, and while they marvel at these things, (and) while they weep for the fate of their friends, that old house, small even for two masters, is turned into a temple: columns replaced the forked beams, the thatch grows golden and seems (to become) a roof of gold, and the doors (seem) engraved and the ground (seems) covered with marble.**

**18 chunks. 9 points total, ½ point each. Round up to nearest whole point.**

| | |
|---|---|
| *tantum aberant summo* | **they were only so far away from the top** |
| *quantum semel ... sagitta* | **as an arrow once** |
| *ire ... missa potest* | **sent is able to go** |
| *flexere oculos* | **they turned their eyes** |
| *et ... cetera prospiciunt* | **and see/look at the rest** |
| *mersa palude* | **flooded with a swamp** |
| *tantum sua tecta manere* | **only their house remains** |
| *dumque ea mirantur* | **and while they marvel/are marveling at these things** |
| *dum deflent fata suorum* | **while they weep/are weeping for the fates of their friends** |
| *illa vetus ... casa* | **that old house** |

| | |
|---|---|
| *dominis etiam . . . parva duobus* | small even for two masters |
| *vertitur in templum* | is turned into a temple |
| *furcas subiere columnae* | columns replaced the forked beams |
| *stramina flavescunt* | the straw/thatch grows golden |
| *aurataque tecta videntur* | and the roof seems golden/to be of gold |
| *caelataeque fores* | and the doors (seem) engraved |
| *adopertaque . . . tellus* | and the floor/ground (seems) covered over |
| *marmore* | with marble |

## Short Analysis Questions

1. Explain how the meter of line 686 reinforces the meaning of the line.

   **The only dactyl in the first four feet of the line occurs over the word *celer* referring to the goose. The heavily spondaic phrase, *tardos aetate*, refers to the slow, old couple.**

2. Briefly describe, without translating word for word, what is happening in lines 684– 688 (*unicus . . . deos*).

   **The couple prepares to slaughter their sole goose for their guests, however the goose flees to the gods as though to ask for a stay of execution.**

3. In describing the wine bowl filling up of its own accord, Ovid uses a striking alliteration in line 680. Write out and explain the Latin that expresses the alliteration.

   ***sponte sua per seque vident succrescere vina.* The repetition of the "s" sounds draws attention to this miraculous occurrence.**

### Essay *Suggested time: 20 minutes*

In this story of piety and loyalty to the gods we see the magnanimous spirits of Philemon and Baucis contrasted with the poverty of their daily existence. In an essay, evaluate this story as a contrast between the two extremes in the lives of these two characters. Can we truly call them fortunate?

Support your assertions with references drawn from **throughout** lines 616–724. All Latin words must be copied or their line numbers provided, AND they must be translated or paraphrased closely enough so that it is clear you understand the Latin. It is your responsibility to convince your reader that you are basing your conclusions on the Latin text and not merely on a general recollection of the passage. Direct your answer to the question; do not merely summarize the passage. Please write your essay on a separate piece of paper.

**The question asks the students to discuss the contrasts of greatness of spirit and poverty of daily life and to determine whether Philemon and Baucis are truly fortunate. The best essays will formulate an argument that demonstrates that, in the eyes of the gods and the speaker Lelex, the elderly couple is fortunate both in their lives and in the manner of their deaths. Students will need to choose passages such as lines 627–636 or 689–703 to show the combination of generosity and poverty and lines 704–724 to illustrate how truly fortunate the elderly couple was.**

6 – A fully developed argument that addresses the contrast and illustrates it with aptly cited Latin passages and that argues that fortune is based on greatness of spirit rather than wealth.

5 – Also a well-developed essay that shows how the contrast reinforces the notion that the couple are truly fortunate, though one that fails to develop its arguments fully. Latin passages are well-chosen and correctly cited.

4 – A competent analytical response but one that does not cite sufficient evidence from the text in support of its arguments.

3 – A weak essay. The Latin citations are inappropriate and poorly cited. There is little or no analysis of the passage. Or, the student shows perception of the meaning of the passage, but does not cite Latin to support his points.

2 – A general, non-focused essay. There is no coherent discussion and the Latin passages are not accurate or appropriate.

1 – A response that lacks coherence and has no central argument. The essay does not demonstrate an understanding of the poem.

0 – The response is irrelevant to the topic or incorrect, or merely restates the question without any analysis.

## Scansion

Scan the following lines.

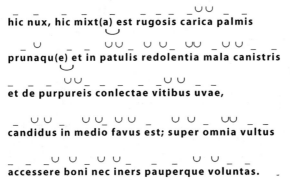

*Metamorphoses 8.674–678*

# Vocabulary

Below you will find a list of high-frequency words you have encountered in your recent readings. For all the words you know, write out full dictionary entries, including English meanings, and put a √ mark in the left-hand column to show you have already committed these words to memory. For any words you do not yet know, write out the dictionary entries using the end glossary and learn them as soon as possible.

√

1. _____ *agō* _____

2. _____ *ars* _____

3. _____ *coepī* _____

4. _____ *crēdō* _____

5. _____ *dux* _____

6. _____ *eō* _____

7. _____ *flāvus* _____

8. _____ *flectō* _____

9. _____ *haereō* _____

10. _____ *iaceō* _____

11. _____ *ignārus* _____

12. _____ *licet* _____

13. _____ *lignum* _____

14. _____ *molliō* _____

15. _____ *nātus* _____

16. _____ *nōtus* _____

17. _____ *novus* _____

18. _____ *nox* _____

19. _____ *oculus* _____

20. _____ *ops* _____

21. _____ *optō* _____

22. ____ *ordō* _____

23. ____ *osculum* _____

24. ____ *pateō* _____

25. ____ *pater* _____

26. ____ *pendeō* _____

27. ____ *perdō* _____

28. ____ *pēs* _____

29. ____ *sol* _____

30. ____ *tectum* _____

31. ____ *valeō* _____

32. ____ *verus* _____

33. ____ *vōs* _____

# PYGMALION
# METAMORPHOSES 10.238–266

"Sunt tamen obscenae Venerem Propoetides ausae
esse negare deam; pro quo sua numinis ira
240 corpora cum fama primae vulgasse feruntur,
utque pudor cessit, sanguisque induruit oris,
in rigidum parvo silicem discrimine versae.
"Quas quia Pygmalion aevum per crimen agentis
viderat, offensus vitiis, quae plurima menti
245 femineae natura dedit, sine coniuge caelebs
vivebat thalamique diu consorte carebat.
interea niveum mira feliciter arte
sculpsit ebur formamque dedit, qua femina nasci
nulla potest, operisque sui concepit amorem.
250 virginis est verae facies, quam vivere credas,
et, si non obstet reverentia, velle moveri:
ars adeo latet arte sua. miratur et haurit
pectore Pygmalion simulati corporis ignes.
saepe manus operi temptantes admovet, an sit
255 corpus an illud ebur, nec adhuc ebur esse fatetur.
oscula dat reddique putat loquiturque tenetque
et credit tactis digitos insidere membris
et metuit, pressos veniat ne livor in artus,
et modo blanditias adhibet, modo grata puellis
260 munera fert illi conchas teretesque lapillos
et parvas volucres et flores mille colorum
liliaque pictasque pilas et ab arbore lapsas
Heliadum lacrimas; ornat quoque vestibus artus,
dat digitis gemmas, dat longa monilia collo,
265 aure leves bacae, redimicula pectore pendent:
cuncta decent; nec nuda minus formosa videtur.

## Short Answer Questions

Line 239     What is the form of *negare*? **present infinitive active**

What is the use of that form? **complementary to *ausae sunt* (line 238)**

What is the case and use of *ira*? **ablative of cause**

Line 240     What is the case and use of *primae*? **predicate nominative plural modifying subject of *feruntur* (with an understood [*esse*])**

Line 243      What is the case and use of *agentis?* **accusative modifying *quas***

Line 246      What is the case and use of *consorte?* **ablative of separation with *carebat***

Line 248      What is the form of *nasci?* **present infinitive active (of *nascor*, deponent)**

              What is the use of that form? **complementary with *potest* (line 249)**

Lines 250–251 What is the form of *credas* and *obstet?* **present subjunctive active**

              What is the use of that form? **future less vivid condition**

Line 251      What is the form of *velle?* **present infinitive active**

              What is the use of that form? **indirect discourse**

Line 254      What is the case and use of *operi?* **dative with compound verb (*admovet*)**

Line 257      What is the form of *insidere?* **present infinitive active**

              What is the use of that form? **indirect statement**

Line 260      What is the case and use of *illi?* **dative, indirect object of *fert***

# Multiple Choice Questions *Suggested time: 12 minutes*

1.  In lines 238–242, we learn that the Propoetides were turned to stone because
    a.  they have dared to challenge Venus
    b.  they had hearts of stone
    c.  **they denied the divinity of Venus**
    d.  they showed no sense of shame

2.  The phrase *parvo . . . discrimine* (line 242) indicates
    a.  **that the Propoetides were nearly stone already**
    b.  that it took a lot to transform the Propoetides
    c.  that prostitution had made the Propoetides hard hearted
    d.  that people without shame are like stone

3.  When the poet writes in lines 244–245 that nature gives many vices to the female mind he is guilty of
    a.  litotes
    b.  **hyperbole**
    c.  irony
    d.  pleonasm

4.  The statement *ars adeo latet arte sua* (line 252) is best translated
    a.  to such an extent does its own art lie concealed
    b.  **to such an extent is his art concealed by his skill**
    c.  his own art conceals its art.
    d.  he conceals his art to a great extent.

5. In line 256 the subject of *reddi* is:

   a. Pygmalion (understood)

   **b. *oscula* (line 256)**

   c. *ebur* (line 255)

   d. *illud* (line 255)

6. The best translation for *tactis digitos insidere membris* (line 257) is

   a. that his fingers sank and touched the limbs

   b. that he touched the limbs with his fingers

   **c. that his fingers sank into the limbs when he touched them**

   d. that he sank his fingers into the touched limbs

7. In line 258, *veniat* is subjunctive because it occurs in a clause that expresses

   a. a condition

   **b. a fear**

   c. an indirect question

   d. purpose

8. In line 264, the figure of speech employed is

   a. alliteration

   **b. anaphora**

   c. personification

   d. onomatopoeia

9. In line 266, *nec nuda minus formosa videtur* means

   a. that the ivory statue is just as beautiful unclothed

   **b. that the ivory statue is more beautiful unclothed**

   c. that the ivory statue is less beautiful unclothed

   d. that the beautiful ivory statue is not unclothed

10. In line 266, *cuncta* refers to

   a. the statue

   b. the garlands

   c. the jewels

   **d. his gifts**

# Translation *Suggested time: 20 minutes*

Translate the passage below as literally as possible.

"Sunt tamen obscenae Venerem Propoetides ausae
esse negare deam; pro quo sua numinis ira
corpora cum fama primae vulgasse feruntur,
utque pudor cessit, sanguisque induruit oris,
5     in rigidum parvo silicem discrimine versae.

"Quas quia Pygmalion aevum per crimen agentis
viderat, offensus vitiis, quae plurima menti
femineae natura dedit, sine coniuge caelebs
vivebat thalamique diu consorte carebat.

*Metamorphoses 10.238–246*

**18 chunks. 9 points total, ½ point each. Round up to nearest whole point.**

**However, the polluted Propoetides dared to deny that Venus was a goddess; for which through the anger of the divine power they are said [to have been] the first to have prostituted their bodies along with their reputation and when their modesty ceased, and the blood of [each] face became hardened, [they are said] to have been changed with little difference into rigid stone.**

**"Whom because Pygmalion had seen them [the daughters of Propoetis] spending their lives in crime, offended by their vices, which nature has given most plentifully to the female mind, he lived as a bachelor without a wife and for a long time lacked a partner for his bedroom.**

| | |
|---|---|
| *tamen* | **however** |
| *obscenae Propoetides* | **the polluted/foul Propoetides** |
| *sunt . . . ausae . . . negare* | **dared to deny** |
| *Venerem esse deam* | **that Venus was a goddess** |
| *pro quo . . . numinis ira* | **for which through the anger of the divine power** |
| *feruntur primae vulgasse* | **they are said [to have been] the first to have prostituted** |
| *sua . . . corpora cum fama* | **their bodies along with their reputation** |
| *utque pudor cessit* | **and as/when their modesty ceased** |
| *sanguisque induruit oris* | **and the blood of [each] face hardened** |
| *in rigidum . . . silicem . . . versae* | **[they were] turned into rigid stone** |
| *parvo discrimine* | **with little difference** |
| *Quas quia Pygmalion . . . agentis viderat* | **Whom since Pygmalion had seen them leading/spending** |
| *aevum per crimen* | **their lives/life in crime/evil** |
| *offensus vitiis* | **having been offended by their vices** |
| *quae plurima . . . natura dedit* | **which nature has given most plentifully/which nature has given very much** |
| *menti femineae* | **to the female mind/mind of the female** |
| *sine coniuge caelebs vivebat* | **he lived as a bachelor without a wife** |
| *thalamique diu consorte carebat* | **and for a long time lacked a partner for his bedroom** |

# Short Analysis Questions

1. Why is the transformation of the Propoetides into stone (line 242) appropriate?

   **Because the daughters of Propoetus had denied that Venus was a goddess and as a punishment had lost all shame, their blood hardened in response. As their modesty left them, their hearts and souls grew hard until they were as unfeeling stone.**

2. What conclusion did Pygmalion draw from the crimes of the Propoetides?

   **He believed that all women were wicked like the Propoetides and thus lived as a bachelor.**

3. a. Translate *virginis est verae facies, quam vivere credas* (line 250).

   **"It had the appearance of a real maiden who you would think was alive."**

   b. What is the effect of the poet's second person singular use of *credas*?

   **The poet makes the reader a viewer of the statue along with Pygmalion. This makes the story more alive for the reader.**

4. Give five examples in English of how Pygmalion treated his statue as if it were a real woman even before he gave it gifts.

   a. **He kissed the statue and thought it kissed him back. (line 256)**

   b. **He spoke to the statue. (line 256)**

   c. **He believed that his fingers sunk into the statue. (line 257)**

   d. **He was afraid that he would bruise if he touched it. (line 258)**

   e. **He complimented the statue. (line 259)**

# PYGMALION
# METAMORPHOSES 10.267–297

conlocat hanc stratis concha Sidonide tinctis
adpellatque tori sociam adclinataque colla
mollibus in plumis, tamquam sensura, reponit.
270 "Festa dies Veneris tota celeberrima Cypro
venerat, et pandis inductae cornibus aurum
conciderant ictae nivea cervice iuvencae,
turaque fumabant, cum munere functus ad aras
constitit et timide 'si, di, dare cuncta potestis,
275 sit coniunx, opto,' non ausus 'eburnea virgo'
dicere Pygmalion 'similis mea' dixit 'eburnae.'
sensit, ut ipsa suis aderat Venus aurea festis,
vota quid illa velint et, amici numinis omen,
flamma ter accensa est apicemque per aera duxit.
280 ut rediit, simulacra suae petit ille puellae
incumbensque toro dedit oscula: visa tepere est;
admovet os iterum, manibus quoque pectora temptat:
temptatum mollescit ebur positoque rigore
subsidit digitis ceditque, ut Hymettia sole
285 cera remollescit tractataque pollice multas
flectitur in facies ipsoque fit utilis usu.
dum stupet et dubie gaudet fallique veretur,
rursus amans rursusque manu sua vota retractat.
corpus erat! saliunt temptatae pollice venae.
290 tum vero Paphius plenissima concipit heros
verba, quibus Veneri grates agat, oraque tandem
ore suo non falsa premit dataque oscula virgo
sensit et erubuit timidumque ad lumina lumen
attollens pariter cum caelo vidit amantem.
295 coniugio, quod fecit, adest dea, iamque coactis
cornibus in plenum noviens lunaribus orbem
illa Paphon genuit, de qua tenet insula nomen."

## Short Answer Questions

Line 267    What is the case and use of *concha*?  **ablative of means**

Line 269    What is the the form of *sensura*?  **future active participle (of *sentio*)**

What does *sensura* modify?  **colla (line 268)**

Translate *sensura*.  **"as if it could feel (as if about to feel)"**

Line 274 What is the case and use of *di*? **vocative, direct address**

Line 278 What is the form of *velint*? **third person plural present subjunctive active**

     What is the use of that form? **indirect question**

Line 281 What is the form of *incumbens*? **present active participle**

     What does *incumbens* modify? **ille (line 280)**

Line 283 How is the form *posito rigore* used? **ablative absolute**

     Translate *posito rigore*. **"when its stiffness had been put aside"**

Line 286 What is the case and use of *usu*? **ablative of means**

Line 289 What is the form of *temptatae*? **perfect passive participle**

     What word does it modify? **venae**

Line 291 What is the case and use of *quibus*? **ablative of means**

     What is the antecedent of *quibus*? **verba**

     Lines 295–296 How is the form of the two words *coactis . . . lunaribus* used? **ablative absolute**

     Translate *coactis lunaribus*. **"when the moon had gathered together"**

## Multiple Choice Questions *Suggested time: 12 minutes*

1. In line 267, *stratis . . . tinctis* is an ablative of
  a. means
  b. comparison
  **c. place where**
  d. manner

2. In lines 275–276, Pygmalion prays for a wife who is
  a. as perfect as his ivory maiden
  b. better than his ivory maiden
  **c. like his ivory maiden**
  d. unlike his ivory maiden

3. Line 279 (*flamma . . . duxit*) is best translated as
  **a. three times the flame burnt up and the flame tip leapt up through the air**
  b. three times the flame was lifted and led its tip through the air
  c. three times he lifted the flame, and led its tip through the air
  d. he lifted the flame into the air three times

4. Lines 280–281 form a
  a. chiasmus
  **b. tricolon crescendo**
  c. synchesis
  d. zeugma

5. The poet illustrates Pygmalion's confusion in line 287 by employing a(n)

    **a. oxymoron**
        b. hyperbaton

    c. polysyndeton
        d. irony

6. Pygmalion in line 289

    a. leaps with delight
        **b. takes the statue's pulse**

    c. is tempted
        d. touches the body

7. The statue blushes in line 293 because

    a. she is naked
        **b. Pygmalion kisses her**

    c. she is afraid
        d. Pygmalion's kisses are false

8. The goddess attends the wedding in line 295 because

    a. she performed a miracle
        b. it is held at her city

    **c. Pygmalion believes in her and her powers**
        d. the statue is her child

9. In line 297 *illa* refers to

    a. Venus
        b. a child

    **c. Pygmalion's wife**
        d. the statue

10. Line 297 (*illa . . . nomen*) is best translated

    **a. she gave birth to Paphos, a child from whom the island takes its name**
        b. she gave birth to Paphos, a boy from whom the island takes its name

    c. she gave birth to Paphos, a girl from whom the island takes its name
        d. she who gave her name to the island, gave birth to Paphos

# Translation *Suggested time: 15 minutes*

Translate the passage below as literally as possible.

> "Festa dies Veneris tota celeberrima Cypro
> venerat, et pandis inductae cornibus aurum
> conciderant ictae nivea cervice iuvencae,
> turaque fumabant, cum munere functus ad aras
> 5    constitit et timide 'si, di, dare cuncta potestis,
> sit coniunx, opto,' non ausus 'eburnea virgo'
> dicere Pygmalion 'similis mea' dixit 'eburnae.'

*Metamorphoses 10.270–277*

"The most famous festival day of Venus in all Cyprus had come and heifers, covered on their bent horns with gold, had fallen, struck on their snowy neck, and incense was smoking, and, having performed his rite at the altars, Pygmalion stood and said fearfully, 'If, gods, you can give all things, I wish my wife to be,' (not daring to say 'my ivory maiden') 'like my ivory [maiden].'

**18 chunks. 9 points total, ½ point each. Round up to nearest whole point.**

| | |
|---|---|
| *festa dies Veneris... venerat* | the holiday/sacred day of Venus had come/festival day |
| *celeberrima* | the most festive |
| *tota... Cypro* | in all of Cyprus |
| *et... inductae... aurum... iuvencae* | and heifers covered in gold |
| *pandis... cornibus* | on their spreading horns |
| *conciderant* | had fallen |
| *ictae nivea cervice* | struck on their snow white neck |
| *turaque fumabant* | and the incense was smoking |
| *cum munere functus* | when having performed his duty / rite |
| *ad aras constititPygmalim* | Pygmalion stood at the altars |
| *et timide... dixit* | and fearfully/timidly/shyly Pygmalion said |
| *si di... potestis* | if gods you are able/can |
| *dare cuncta* | (to) give/(to) grant all things |
| *sit coniunx* | that my wife be |
| *opto* | I desire |
| *non ausus... dicere* | not daring to say |
| *eburnea virgo... mea* | my ivory maiden |
| *similis... eburnae* | like/similar to my ivory [maiden] |

# Short Analysis Questions

1. What are the central ritual events at the annual festival for Venus at Cyprus as described in lines 270–273?

   a. **the sacrifice of heifers**

   b. **the burning of incense**

   c. **the placing of gifts at the altar of the goddess**

2. What is the significance of the incident described in line 279?

   **This means that the goddess will intervene and answer Pygmalion's prayer.**

3. a. Translate *ut Hymettia sole/ cera remollescit tractataque pollice multas/ flectitur in facies ipsoque fit utilis usu* (lines 284–286).

   **"As Hymettian wax melts from the sun, and molded by the thumb, is turned to many forms, and becomes useful by its very use."**

   b. Explain two parallels that show why this simile is particularly appropriate to describe the statue coming to life. Cite the Latin for your examples.

   1. **Pygmalion's heat softens the statue (*mollescit ebur*) as the sun softens the wax (*Hymettia cera remollescit*.)**

   2. **The wax is softened by handling with the thumb (*tractataque pollice*) just as the statue gives way to Pygmalion's fingers (*subsidit digitis*).**

## Essay *Suggested time: 20 minutes*

In the story of Pygmalion, the poet offers an antithesis between the transformations of the Propoetides and the statue. What is this antithesis and how is it developed in the passage? Write an essay in which you discuss how and why the two transformations are contrasted.

Support your assertions with references drawn from **throughout** lines 238–297. All Latin words must be copied or their line numbers provided, AND they must be translated or paraphrased closely enough so that it is clear you understand the Latin. It is your responsibility to convince your reader that you are basing your conclusions on the Latin text and not merely on a general recollection of the passage. Direct your answer to the question; do not merely summarize the passage. Please write your essay on a separate piece of paper.

**The question asks the students to compare the transformations of the Propoetides into stone with that of the statue turned to a living woman and to argue as to the appropriateness of the contrast of this particular pair of transformations to show the punishment of the impious prostitutes and the reward of the chaste and pious Pygmalion. Among the Latin cited might be lines 238–242, 243–246, and 280–289. A very strong essay might also consider how Ovid typically undermines this simple contrast by showing Pygmalion as not entirely chaste because of his erotic attraction for his statue.**

6 – A fully developed essay supported by well-chosen and correctly cited Latin examples. The student will argue how and why the contrasting metamorphoses are presented and may also consider the irony of the depiction of Pygmalion himself.

5 – A strong essay that uses appropriate Latin examples and develops a convincing, though not fully developed argument.

4 – A competent essay that analyses the contrast but does not have sufficient Latin examples to support the argument.

3 – A weak essay. The Latin citations are inappropriate and poorly cited. There is little or no analysis of the passage. Or, the student shows perception of the meaning of the passage, but does not cite Latin to support his points.

2 – A general, non-focused essay. There is no coherent discussion and the Latin passages are not accurate or appropriate.

1 – A response that lacks coherence and has no central argument. The essay does not demonstrate an understanding of the poem.

0 – The response is irrelevant to the topic or incorrect, or merely restates the question without any analysis.

# Scansion

Scan the following lines.

$$\_ \quad \_ \quad \_ \quad \_ \quad \_ \quad \cup\cup \quad \_ \quad \cup\cup \quad - \quad \cup \quad \cup \quad \_ \quad \_$$
et, si non obstet reverentia, velle moveri:

$$\_ \quad \cup\cup \quad \cup\cup \quad \_ \quad \cup \quad \cup\_ \quad \_ \quad \_ \cup \quad \cup \quad \_ \quad \_$$
ars adeo latet arte sua. miratur et haurit

$$\_ \quad \cup\cup \quad \_ \quad \cup\cup\_ \quad \cup \quad \cup \quad \_ \quad \_ \quad \_ \quad \cup\cup \quad \_ \quad \_$$
pectore Pygmalion simulati corporis ignes.

$$\_ \quad \cup \quad \cup \quad \_ \quad \cup\cup \quad \_ \quad \_ \quad \_ \quad \_ \quad \_ \quad \cup \quad \cup \quad \_ \quad \_$$
saepe manus operi temptantes admovet, an sit

*Metamorphoses 10.251–254*

# Vocabulary

1. Make a list of all the gifts that Pygmalion offered to his ivory statue. Beside each Latin word provide line references in parentheses. Give the dictionary entry and meaning for each noun.

   a. *concha, -ae* (f.) shell (line 260)

   b. *lapillus, -i* (m.) small stone (line 260)

   c. *volucris, -cris* (f.) a bird (line 261)

   d. *lilium, -i* (n.) lily (line 262)

   e. *pila, -ae* (f.) ball (line 262)

   f. *gemma, -ae* (f.) jewel, gem (line 264)

   g. *monile, -is* (n.) necklace (line 264)

   h. *baca, -ae* (f.) pearl (line 265)

   i. *redimiculum, -i* (n.) band, wreath, garland (line 265)

2. Make a list of all the verbs that describe touching or feeling. Give the dictionary entry and meaning for each verb. Cite each verb only once. Provide line references in parentheses beside each verb.

   a. *insideo, -ere, -sedi, -sessum* sink in, become embedded (line 257)

   b. *premo, -ere, -ssi, -ssum* to press on, push, to cover (line 258)

   c. *sentio, -ire, sensi, sensum* to feel, sense (line 269)

   d. *tempto, -are, -avi, -atum* to try, attept, handle, touch, feel (line 283)

   e. *tracto, -are, -avi, -atum* to handle, manage (line 285)

   f. *retracto, -are, -avi, -atum* to handle, feel for a second time (line 288)

3. Make a list of all the parts of the body found in the passage. Beside each Latin word provide line references in parentheses. Give the dictionary entry and meaning for each noun.

   **(Let students know to include the repeated uses of the body parts.)**

   a. *os, oris* (n.) face (line 241)

   b. *pectus, -oris* (n.) chest, breast, heart (line 253)

   c. *manus, -us* (f.) hand (line 254)

   d. *digitus, -i* (m.) finger, toe (line 257)

   e. *membrum, -i* (n.) limb of the body (line 257)

   f. *artus, -us* (m.) limb of the body (line 258)

   g. *collum, -i* (n.) neck (line 264)

h. *auris, -is* (f.) ear (line 265)

i. *cervix, -vicis* (f.) neck (line 272)

j. *os* (see a.) (line 282)

k. *manus* (see c.) (line 282)

l. *pectus* (see b.) (line 282)

m. *digitus* (see d.) (line 284)

n. *pollex, -icis* (m.) thumb (line 285)

o. *manus* (see c.) (line 288)

p. *pollex* (see n.) (line 289)

q. *os* (see a.) (line 292)

r. *lumen, -inis* (n.) eye (line 293)

# APPENDICES
# A AND B

# APPENDIX A
# PRACTICE EXAM 1

## Question 1 *Suggested time: 20 minutes*

carmine nomen habent exterrita cornibus Io
et quam fluminea lusit adulter ave
quaeque super pontum simulato vecta iuvenco
virginea tenuit cornua vara manu.

*Amores* 1.3.21–24

ardet in abducta Briseide magnus Achilles
(dum licet, Argeas frangite, Troes, opes);
Hector ab Andromaches complexibus ibat ad arma,
et galeam capiti quae daret, uxor erat;
5    summa ducum, Atrides visa Priameide fertur
Maenadis effusis obstipuisse comis.
Mars quoque deprensus fabrilia vincula sensit:
notior in caelo fabula nulla fuit.

*Amores* 1.9.33–40

In each of the passages above, Ovid uses lists of mythological characters to support an argument that he is trying to make. Write an essay in which you examine each of the passages and compare how successfully his mythological examples support his argument.

Support your assertions with references drawn from **throughout** both passages. All Latin words must be copied or their line numbers provided, AND they must be translated or paraphrased closely enough so that it is clear you understand the Latin. It is your responsibility to convince your reader that you are basing your conclusions on the Latin text and not merely on a general recollection of the passage. Direct your answer to the question; do not merely summarize the passage. Please write your essay on a separate piece of paper.

**In this essay students are given two passages to consider—one from *Amores* 1.3 and one from *Amores* 1.9. Students should set the stage for each of these excerpts explaining the context, the characters, and the argument Ovid is trying to make with the use of these mythological characters. The analysis should note the ironic use of the examples in *Amores* 1.3; that in support of his claim of eternal fidelity, Ovid has chosen as examples three women whom he deceived and raped. In the second passage students should note the appropriateness of choosing mythological characters who exemplify the argument that warriors and lovers share the same purpose and that both are men of action, not indolence. The essay should focus on analysis of Ovid's effectiveness in employing these mythological characters with reference to specific Latin words or phrases to support all points made.**

6 – A well-thought out essay that examines how successfully Ovid's mythological examples support his argument. The essay is makes generous use of relevant references from the Latin in both passages to support the comparison. The essay should reveal the extent to which the student understands the undercurrent in Ovid's use of the characters he chooses.

5 – A strong essay that shows that the student recognizes the characters mentioned and understands Ovid's choice in using them. Although the piece has good analysis, it is not so fully developed nor so supported with references to the text as a 6 paper. Latin references are properly cited. The essay reflects familiarity with the poem.

4 – An adequate essay that recognizes the two passages but weakly understands Ovid's purpose in employing them in their contexts. There may be uneven development. Although limited in quantity, the essay includes accurate and relevant references in responding to the two passages. The Latin cited is generally accurate however the discussion may be more descriptive than analytical.

3 – A limited attempt to respond to the question. The essay relies too heavily on summary rather than analysis. The Latin support is weak and perhaps inappropriate. The student may demonstrate an understanding of the passages but cites no Latin to support the answer.

2 – An unfocused attempt to answer the question. The essay contains vague statements about the passages or Ovid's poetry in general. The Latin cited shows lack of comprehension.

1 – A response that, although it may recognize the poetry, does not contain a substantive argument.

0 – A restatement of the question or an essay which shows no relevance to the passages quoted.

## Question 2 *Suggested time: 15 minutes*

Translate the passage below as literally as possible.

> quis nisi vel miles vel amans et frigora noctis
> et denso mixtas perferet imbre nives?
> mittitur infestos alter speculator in hostes,
> in rivale oculos alter, ut hoste, tenet.
> 5    ille graves urbes, hic durae limen amicae
> obsidet; hic portas frangit, at ille fores.

*Amores* 1.9.15–20

**Who, if not the soldier or lover, will endure the cold of night and snows mixed with dense rain showers? The one is sent as a spy into the hostile enemy, the other one holds his eyes on his rival, as though an enemy. The former besieges important cities, the latter the threshold of his hardhearted mistress; this one breaks down city gates, that one doors.**

**18 chunks. 9 points total, ½ point each. Round up to nearest whole point.**

| | |
|---|---|
| *quis nisi* | **who if not/unless/except** |
| *vel miles vel amans* | **either the/a soldier or the/a lover** |
| *et frigora noctis* | **both the cold of the night** |
| *denso . . . imbre* | **with the thick rain storm** |
| *et mixtas . . . nives* | **and snows mixed (with)** |
| *perferet* | **will endure** |
| *mittitur . . . alter* | **the one is sent** |
| *infestos . . . in hostes* | **into the hostile enemy** |
| *speculator* | **as a spy** |
| *in rivale* | **on/against his rival** |
| *oculos* | **his eyes** |
| *alter . . . tenet* | **the other one holds** |
| *ut hoste* | **as an enemy** |
| *ille . . . obsidet* | **the former besieges** |
| *graves urbes* | **important cities** |
| *hic durae limen amicae* | **the latter the threshold of his hard-hearted mistress** |
| *hic portas frangit* | **this one breaks down city gates** |
| *at ille fores* | **but that one the doors [of a house]** |

## Question 3 *Suggested time: 15 minutes*

Plura locuturum timido Peneia cursu
fugit cumque ipso verba inperfecta reliquit,
tum quoque visa decens; nudabant corpora venti,
obviaque adversas vibrabant flamina vestes,
5   et levis inpulsos retro dabat aura capillos,
auctaque forma fuga est. sed enim non sustinet ultra
perdere blanditias iuvenis deus, utque monebat
ipse Amor, admisso sequitur vestigia passu.

*Metamorphoses* 1.525–532

1.   Discuss the significance of the word order of line 4.

**This line consists of a verb (*vibrabant*) in the center, surrounded by an adjective/noun pair (*obviaque flamina / adversas vestes*) in interlocked word order—a golden line mimicking the blowing wind.**

2.   a.   Translate *auctaque forma fuga est* (line 6).

**"Her beauty was increased by her flight."**

     b.   Citing the Latin and translating your choices, list the three ways in lines 3–6 that the action in *auctaque forma fuga est* (line 6) is accomplished.

**nudabant corpora venti—the winds lay naked her body**

**obviaque adversas vibrabant flamina vestes—the opposing breezes were ruffling her clothing which was standing in the way**

**levis inpulsos retro dabat aura capillos—the breeze was causing her blown hair to go backwards**

3.   In line 1, to whom does *locuturum* refer?

**Apollo**

# PRACTICE EXAM 2

## Question 1 *Suggested time: 20 minutes*

omnia possideat, non possidet aera Minos."
dixit et ignotas animum dimittit in artes
naturamque novat. nam ponit in ordine pennas
a minima coeptas, longam breviore sequenti,
5   ut clivo crevisse putes: sic rustica quondam
fistula disparibus paulatim surgit avenis;
tum lino medias et ceris alligat imas
atque ita conpositas parvo curvamine flectit,
ut veras imitetur aves.

*Metamorphoses* 8.187–195

interea niveum mira feliciter arte
sculpsit ebur formamque dedit, qua femina nasci
nulla potest, operisque sui concepit amorem.
virginis est verae facies, quam vivere credas,
5   et, si non obstet reverentia, velle moveri:
ars adeo latet arte sua.

*Metamorphoses* 10.247–252

In the above two passages, Ovid describes two artists and their work. In an essay, consider the craft of the artist, the purpose for which the work of art is created, and the outcome of the artist's production.

Support your assertions with references drawn from **throughout** both passages. All Latin words must be copied or their line numbers provided, AND they must be translated or paraphrased closely enough so that it is clear you understand the Latin. It is your responsibility to convince your reader that you are basing your conclusions on the Latin text and not merely on a general recollection of the passage. Direct your answer to the question; do not merely summarize the passage. Please write your essay on a separate piece of paper.

**In this essay students are asked to consider the skill, purpose, and product of the artist. In so doing, the student should explain the impetus behind the work of art, the creative process described in the passages, the result of the artist's work, and even comment on the application of all this to the art of the poet himself. The essay should contain specific reference to Latin phrases and vocabulary from both passages and should be organized to enhance the argument.**

**6 – A well-organized analysis of the work of the artist portrayed in each passage and perhaps by extension to the work of the poet creating these passages. The student makes ample reference to specific aspects of the Latin text to support his analysis and his position. The Latin is appropriate and cited equally from both passages.**

5 – A strong essay that reveals the intent and the product of the artist. The essay either lacks the depth of a 6 or is limited to the passages at hand. Latin references are properly cited. The essay reflects familiarity with the passages.

4 – A competent response which discusses the two artists and their work. There may be uneven development. Although limited in quantity, the essay includes accurate and relevant references in responding to the topic. The discussion may be more descriptive than analytical.

3 – An essay that recognizes the passages and explains them literally but offers little analysis. It may fail to cite sufficient Latin or it may favor one passage over the other.

2 – A weak essay that may show some familiarity with the passages but is unable to elucidate any artistry or significance from the passages.

1 – The student makes an attempt to answer the question but can bring no understanding of the Latin to bear on the argument.

0 – A response that shows no comprehension or identification of the passages at hand.

## Question 2 *Suggested time: 15 minutes*

Translate the passage below as literally as possible:

> fissus erat tenui rima, quam duxerat olim,
> cum fieret, paries domui communis utrique.
> id vitium nulli per saecula longa notatum—
> quid non sentit amor?—primi vidistis amantes
> 5    et vocis fecistis iter, tutaeque per illud
> murmure blanditiae minimo transire solebant.
>
> *Metamorphoses 4.65–70*

A wall, common to both houses, had been split by a thin crack which had developed long ago, when it [the wall] was made. This defect noticed by no one through the long ages—but what does love not perceive?—you lovers first saw it, and you made a way for your voice, and safe endearments used to pass in a very small whisper.

18 chunks. 9 points total, ½ point each. Round up to nearest whole point.

| | |
|---|---|
| *fissus erat* | **it had been split** |
| *tenui rima* | **with a thin crack** |
| *quam duxerat olim* | **which had developed long ago** |
| *cum fieret* | **when it was made** |
| *paries ... communis* | **a wall common** |
| *domui ... utrique* | **to each house** |
| *id vitium* | **this defect** |
| *nulli* | **by no one** |
| *per saecula longa* | **through the long ages** |
| *notatum* | **(had been) noticed** |

| | |
|---|---|
| *quid non sentit amor* | **what does love not sense** |
| *primi ... amantes* | **you lovers for the first time/were the first** |
| *vidistis* | **(you) saw (it)/to see** |
| *et vocis fecistis iter* | **and you made a passage for your voice** |
| *tutaeque ... blanditiae* | **and safe endearments** |
| *per illud* | **through that [space]/it** |
| *murmure ... minimo* | **with the smallest murmuring** |
| *transire solebant* | **were accustomed to pass through** |

## Question 3 *Suggested time: 15 minutes*

> Mantua Vergilio gaudet, Verona Catullo;
>   Paelignae dicar gloria gentis ego,
> quam sua libertas ad honesta coegerat arma,
>   cum timuit socias anxia Roma manus.
> 5   atque aliquis spectans hospes Sulmonis aquosi
>   moenia, quae campi iugera pauca tenent,
> "quae tantum" dicet "potuistis ferre poetam,
>   quantulacumque estis, vos ego magna voco."

*Amores* 3.15.7–14

1.  a. Cite the Latin in which the poet elevates himself to the status of Catullus and Vergil.

    **Paelignae dicar gloria gentis ego**

    b. Write out a translation for the Latin you cited.

    **"I shall be called the glory of the Paelignian race."**

2.  a. Write out the Latin that expresses a chiasmus in line 4.

    **A    B    B    A**
    **socias anxia Roma manus**

    b. What effect does this chiasmus have on the meaning of the line?

    **The chiasmus graphically surrounds anxious Rome with its feared fellow forces.**

3.  In lines 6–8, the poet draws a comparison between great and small.

    a. Write out the Latin that expresses each of these and translate the words.

    **great: *tantum*—so great, *magna*—great**

    **small: *pauca*—small, *quantulacumque*—however small**

    b. What is the purpose of this comparison?

    **This comparison serves to emphasize Ovid's point that although his home town is tiny, it is great because it has produced a poet as great as Ovid.**

# PRACTICE EXAM 3

## Question 1 *Suggested time: 20 minutes*

Colligere incertos et in ordine ponere crines
    docta neque ancillas inter habenda Nape
inque ministeriis furtivae cognita noctis
    utilis et dandis ingeniosa notis,
5    saepe venire ad me dubitantem hortata Corinnam,
    saepe laboranti fida reperta mihi,
accipe et ad dominam peraratas mane tabellas
    perfer et obstantes sedula pelle moras.
nec silicum venae nec durum in pectore ferrum
10    nec tibi simplicitas ordine maior adest;
credibile est et te sensisse Cupidinis arcus:
    in me militiae signa tuere tuae.

                                     *Amores* 1.11.1–12


Flete meos casus: tristes rediere tabellae;
    infelix hodie littera posse negat.
omina sunt aliquid: modo cum discedere vellet,
    ad limen digitos restitit icta Nape.
5    missa foras iterum limen transire memento
    cautius atque alte sobria ferre pedem.

                                       *Amores* 1.12.1–6

In the above two passages, Ovid refers to Corinna's maid Nape. Write an essay in which you examine the characterizations that the poet develops in these two passages. How does the poet create two distinctly different Napes?

Support your assertions with references drawn from **throughout** both passages. All Latin words must be copied or their line numbers provided, AND they must be translated or paraphrased closely enough so that it is clear you understand the Latin. It is your responsibility to convince your reader that you are basing your conclusions on the Latin text and not merely on a general recollection of the passage. Direct your answer to the question; do not merely summarize the passage. Please write your essay on a separate piece of paper.

**This essay asks students to respond to the two characterizations that Ovid creates for the same woman and in doing so to reveal the skill of the poet. The student should first address the Nape as presented in *Amores* 1.11 and cite the many adjectives that compliment the maid in lines 1–8 and from lines 9–12 those phrases that offer further blandishments. The essay should make mention of lines 5–6 of *Amores* 1.12 that offer a thinly-veiled threat suggesting blame on Nape's part for the tablets returning with their unfortunate response.**

6 – A fully-developed essay which discusses how the poet creates two distinct characterizations of Nape. It should make clear the art of the poet in presenting such divergent characterizations of the same person and perhaps by extension to human nature in general. The student makes ample reference to specific aspects of the Latin text to support his analysis and his position. Latin references are properly cited. Even though there may be occasional mistakes, the discussion is coherent and of high quality.

5 – A strong essay that is thought out and executed according to a plan. It should present the contrasting personifications but may lack the depth of analysis or sophistication of a 6. Latin references are properly cited. The essay reflects familiarity with the poem.

4 – A competent essay that understands the question and attempts to discuses how the poet creates two distinct characterizations of Nape. There may be uneven development. Although limited in quantity, the essay includes accurate and relevant references in responding to the topic. The discussion may be more descriptive than analytical.

3 – A limited response that may be unbalanced on contain gross inaccuracies. The essay shows recognition of the passages but is unable to offer any comment or analysis beyond the obvious. The Latin is weak and perhaps misapplied. The answer is descriptive as opposed to analytical.

2 – A weak essay that may show recognition of the passages but is unable to reveal any meaning from them. The Latin cited demonstrates very limited comprehension.

1 – The essay shows lack of comprehension of either the question or the Latin passages. While it may contain some relevant information, no substantive argument is presented. The student demonstrates no understanding of the poem.

0 – An incompetent or irrelevant answer.

## Question 2 *Suggested time: 15 minutes*

Translate the passage below as literally as possible.

> questus eram, pharetra cum protinus ille soluta
> legit in exitium spicula facta meum
> lunavitque genu sinuosum fortiter arcum
> "quod" que "canas, vates, accipe" dixit "opus."
> 5  me miserum! certas habuit puer ille sagittas.
> uror, et in vacuo pectore regnat Amor.

*Amores* 1.1.21–26

I had made my complaint when suddenly he, with quiver undone, selected an arrow designed for my ruin and with great force bent the curved bow with his knee and said, "Accept the task of which you may sing."

Oh, wretched me! That boy possessed accurate arrows. I burn, and Love reigns in my empty breast.

**18 chunks. 9 points total, ½ point each. Round up to nearest whole point.**

| | |
|---|---|
| questus eram | I had made my complaint/had complained |
| pharetra . . . soluta | with loosened quiver |
| cum protinus | when forthwith/immediately |
| ille legit | that boy/he chose |
| spicula facta | arrow/arrows made |
| in exitium . . . meum | for my destruction/ruin |
| lunavitque . . . fortiter | and he bent with great force |
| genu | with his knee |
| sinuosum . . . arcum | the curved bow |
| quod . . . canas vates | that which you may sing of, poet |
| -que . . . dixit | and he said |
| accipe . . . opus | accept the task |
| me miserum | oh wretched me |
| certas . . . sagittas | certain arrows |
| habuit puer ille | that boy had |
| uror | I burn |
| et in vacuo pectore | and in my empty heart/chest |
| regnat Amor | Love rules/governs |

## Question 3 *Suggested time: 15 minutes*

> talia tum placido Saturnius edidit ore:
> 'dicite, iuste senex et femina coniuge iusto
> digna, quid optetis.' cum Baucide pauca locutus
> iudicium superis aperit commune Philemon:
> 5    'esse sacerdotes delubraque vestra tueri
> poscimus, et quoniam concordes egimus annos,
> auferat hora duos eadem, nec coniugis umquam
> busta meae videam, neu sim tumulandus ab illa.'
>
>                      *Metamorphoses* 8.703–710

1. In the above passage Philemon makes three requests of the gods. Write out and translate the Latin for each request.

   a. ***esse sacerdotes*—to be priests (line 5)**

   b. ***delubraque vestra tueri*—to watch over your temples (line 5)**

   c. ***nec coniugis umquam/busta meae videam, neu sim tumulandus ab illa.***
   **May I not ever see the tomb of my wife nor must I be buried away from her. (lines 7–8)**

2. a. In line 1, to whom does Saturnius refer?

   **Jupiter**

    b.  What is the effect of this patronymic?

**It highlights Jupiter's ancestry.**

3.    Write out the Latin for and explain the metonymy in line 4.

**The word *superis* literally means those from above and thus highlights the lofty status of the gods.**

# APPENDIX B
# HIGH-FREQUENCY WORD LIST

The following list contains words which occur **five** or more times in the Ovid AP passages.

**ā, ab** (+ abl.) from

**accipiō, -ere, -cēpī, -ceptum** to receive, accept

**ad** (+ acc.) to, at; by the light of

**aes, aeris** (n.) money, pay

**āiō** to say, assert; reply

**alter . . . alter** the one . . . the other

**amans, -ntis** (m., f.) lover

**amō, -āre, -āvī, -ātum** to love; to fall in love

**amor, -ōris** (m.) love, love affair

**aqua, -ae** (f.) water, sea

**arbor, -oris** (f.) tree

**arma, -ōrum** (n. pl.) arms, weapons; fighting, war

**ars, -tis** (f.) skill, art

**at** (conj.) at least, but, yet; while, whereas

**atque** (conj.) and in fact, and what is more, and indeed, and even

**aura, -ae** (f.) breeze, air

**aut** (conj.) or

**aut . . . aut** either . . . or

**bellum, -ī** (n.) war

**carmen, -minis** (n.) poetry, song

**cēra, -ae** (f.) wax, beeswax

**certus, -a, -um** accurate, precise, sure

**color, -ōris** (m.) color

**corpus, -oris** (n.) body

**cum** (conj.) when; (prep. + abl.) with, along with

**deus, -ī** (m.) god, deity

**dīcō, -ere, dixī, dictum** to say; to appoint, fix

**digitus, -ī** (m.) finger; toe

**dō, dare, dedī, datum** to give; to allow; to cause to go

**dum** (conj.) while

**dux, -cis** (m.) general, leader

**ē, ex** (+ abl.) from

**ebur, -oris** (n.) ivory

**ego** I

**eō, īre, i(v)ī, itum** to go

**et** (conj.) and; also; even

**et . . . et** both . . . and; also

**faciō, -ere, fēcī, factum** to make, do; bring about, inspire; to act; to reveal; to see that

**fallō, -ere, fefellī, falsum** to deceive, trick; to fail; to while away, beguile

**ferō, ferre, tulī, lātum** to tell, relate; to carry, bear, bring

**ferus, -a, -um** fierce, wild

**fugiō, -ere, -ī, -itum** to flee

**habeō, -ēre, -uī, -itum** to have, possess; to hold

**hic, haec, hoc** this, the latter

**hostis, -is** (m.) enemy

**iaceō, -ēre, -uī, -tum** to lie down, lie; to be overthrown

**iam** (adv.) now

**ignis, -is** (m.) fire, star

**ille, illa, illud** that, the former; he, she

**in** (+ acc.) over, affecting; for, towards; into; among; (+ abl.) in, on

**inquam, inquit** to say

**ipse, -a, -um** oneself, itself

**lacertus, -ī** (m.) upper arm

**legō, -ere, lēgī, lectum** to choose, select, pick out; to read

**locus, -ī** (m.) place; open land

longus, -a, -um long, tall

loquor, -quī, -cūtus to speak

magnus, -a, -um great, large

manus, -ūs (f.) hand; armed force, band

medius, -a, -um middle, middle of; between; in half, half; medium, moderate

meus, -a, -um my

mīles, -itis (m.) soldier

miser, -era, -erum wretched, miserable

modo (adv.) just now, recently, lately; just, only

multus, -a, -um much

nātus, -ī (m.) son

nec and . . . not; not even

nimium (adv.) excessively, extremely, very much

nōmen, -minis (n.) name, family name, fame, reputation

nōn (adv.) not

noster, -tra, -trum our

novus, -a, -um new, unfamiliar

nox, -ctis (f.) night

nūdus, -a, -um bare, pure, open, simple; naked, unclothed

nullus, -a, -um no one, nobody, nothing; no; insignificant, trifling

oculus, -ī (m.) eye

omnis, -e each, every, all

opus, -eris (n.) task, undertaking, work, job; need

ordō, -dinis (m.) order; class, rank; a linear arrangement

ōs, ōris (n.) face; mouth

osculum, -ī (n.) mouth, lips; kiss

pārens, -entis (m., f.) ancestor, parent

pater, -tris (m.) father

pectus, -oris (n.) chest, breast

penna, -ae (f.) wing, feather

per (+ acc.) through, throughout

perdō, -ere, -idī, -itum to waste one's effort or time; to destroy

pēs, pedis (m.) foot, metrical foot

petō, -ere, -īvī, -ītum to seek, look for; to seek the hand of in marriage, to court

placeō, -ēre, -uī, -itum (+ dat.) to be pleasing or acceptable

pōnō, -ere, posuī, positum to put, place, arrange; to lay aside, abandon

possum, posse, potuī to be able

puella, -ae (f.) girl, young woman

puer, -ī (m.) boy

quī, quae, quod who, which

quis, quid who? what?

quoque (adv.) also, too

rāmus, -ī (m.) branch

relinquō, -ere, -liquī, -lictum to leave behind

saepe (adv.) often

sed (conj.) but

semper (adv.) always

sentiō, -īre, sensī, sensum to feel, sense

sī (conj.) if

sīc (adv.) thus, in this way, in like manner

sub (+ abl.) under, underneath; at the base of; (+ acc.) at the base of, just at

sum, esse, fuī, futūrus to be

suus, -a, -um his, her, its, their

tabella, -ae (f.) writing tablet

tamen (adv.) nevertheless

tangō, -ere, tetigī, tactum to touch, come in contact with

temptō, -āre, -āvī, -ātum to try, attempt; to handle, touch, feel

teneō, -ēre, -uī, -tum to hold, have; to catch

timidus, -a, -um fearful, apprehensive, timid

tōtus, -a, -um the whole of

tū you (sing.)

tuus, -a, -um your (sing.)

unda, -ae (f.) body of flowing water, river; water

ūnus, -a, -um one; alone

ut (conj.) just as, like; when; in order that; since

vacuus, -a, -um empty, unattached, free, unoccupied

vel (conj.) either . . . or; at any rate

veniō, -īre, vēnī, ventum to come

verbum, -ī (n.) word

vestis, -is (f.) clothing; cloth

virgō, -inis (f.) maiden

volō, velle, voluī to wish for; to wish

vōs you (pl.)

vulnus, -eris (n.) wound, injury

# A COMPLETE VOCABULARY

Words marked with a ~ are also listed in the High-Frequency Word List.

## A

ā (interj.) ah!

~ā, ab (+ abl.) from

~abditus, -a, -um hidden, concealed

abdūcō, -dūcere, -dūxi, -ductum to carry off

abeō, -īre, -iī, -itum to change, be transformed into

absum, -esse, āfuī, āfūtūrus to be missing; to be away from

absūmō, -ere, -sumpsī, -sumptum to use up, squander, spend

ac (conj.) and

accēdō, -ere, -cessī, -cessum to follow in accordance; to be added

accendō, -ere, -dī, -censum to light, ignite; (pass.) to flare up

accingō, -ere, -cinxī, -cinctum to gird, equip

~accipiō, -ere, -cēpī, -ceptum to receive, accept

accommodō, -āre, -āvī, -ātum to fasten on, fit

acer, -eris (n.) maple wood

ācer, ācris, ācre vigorous, energetic

Achillēs, -is (m.) Achilles, Greek hero of the Trojan War

acūtus, -a, -um pointed, sharp

~ad (+ acc.) to, at; by the light of

adclīnō, -āre, -āvī, -ātum to lean or rest on

adcumbō, -ere, -cubuī, -cubitum to recline at table

addūcō, -ere, -dūxī, -ductum to pull taut

adeō, -īre, -iī, -itum to approach

adeō (adv.) especially, extremely, to such a degree

adflō, -āre, -āvī, -ātum to breathe onto, blow onto

adhibeō, -ēre, -uī, -itum to apply

adhūc (adv.) already; yet, as yet, still

adimō, -ere, -ēmī, -emptum to take away

adiuvō, -āre, -iūvī, -iūtum to help, assist

admittō, -ere, -mīsī, -missum to give loose rein to, release, let go

admoveō, -ēre, -mōvī, -mōtum to move or place near to

adnuō, -ere, -uī, -ūtum to nod; to nod in approval

adoleō, -ēre, -uī, adultum to burn

adoperiō, -īre, -uī, -tum to cover over

adpellō, -āre, -āvī, -ātum to call, address, name

adserō, -ere, -uī, -tum to lay claim to

adspergō, -ginis (f.) sprinkling, splashing, scattering

adspiciō, -ere, -spexī, -spectum to observe, behold, catch sight of

adsum, -esse, -fuī, -fūtūrus to be present

adulter, -erī (m.) adulterer

adūrō, -ere, -ussī, -ustum to burn, scorch

adversus, -a, -um opposing, obstructing, standing in the way

aedēs, -is (f.) temple, sanctuary

aemula, -ae (f.) a female imitator

aēnum, -ī (n.) a pot or cauldron made of bronze

aequō, -āre, -āvī, -ātum to make level

aequor, -oris (n.) calm, flat surface of the sea

aequus, -a, -um like; equal; ex aequō equally

āēr, āeris (m.) air

~aes, aeris (n.) money, pay

aestuō, -āre, -āvī, -ātum to seethe; to blaze

aetās, -ātis (f.) age

aethēr, -eris (m.) air, sky

aevum, -ī (n.) lifetime, experience, years of age

affectō, -āre, -āvī, -ātum to aspire to, attempt

agilis, -e active, busy

agitō, -āre, -āvī, -ātum to shake, brandish

agmen, -minis (n.) army

agna, -ae (f.) ewe lamb

**agō, -ere, ēgī, actum** to lead, drive; to deliver, give; spend (time) **quid agam** how am I?

**~āiō** to say, assert, reply

**āla, -ae** (f.) wing

**albus, -a, -um** white, clear, colorless

**āles, -itis** (m.) large bird

**aliquis, aliquid** someone, something

**aliter** (adv.) otherwise, differently

**alligō, -āre, -āvī, -ātum** to tie, fasten

**altē** (adv.) at a great height

**~alter . . . alter** the one . . . the other

**altus, -a, -um** high; deep

**alumnus, -ī** (m.) a "son" in the sense of a product of a particular environment

**alveus, -ī** (m.) a hollowed-out vessel, dish

**~amans, -ntis** (m., f.) lover

**Amathusius, -a, -um** of or pertaining to a town on Cyprus, sacred to Venus

**ambiguum, -ī** (n.) uncertainty, doubt

**ambitiōsus, -a, -um** vain, ambitious, conceited

**ambō, -ae, -ō** both, the two

**amīca, -ae** (f.) mistress

**amictus, -ūs** (m.) cloak

**amīcus, -a, -um** friendly, loving

**~amō, -āre, -āvī, -ātum** to love, fall in love

**~amor, -ōris** (m.) love, love affair

**amplector, -ī, -plexus** to embrace

**an** (conj.) or, or rather; whether

**an . . . an** whether . . . or

**ancilla, -ae** (f.) female slave

**Andromachē, -ēs** (f.) Andromache, wife of Hector

**anhēlitus, -ūs** (m.) gasp, panting

**anīlis, -e** of or pertaining to an old woman

**anima, -ae** (f.) soul, life; breath

**animal, -ālis** (n.) animal

**animus, -ī** (m.) courage, spirit, morale; mind, soul

**annus, -ī** (m.) year

**ansa, -ae** (f.) a handle

**anser, -eris** (m.) goose

**ante** (adv.) previously, once; in front, ahead; (prep. + acc.) before, in front of

**antrum, -ī** (n.) cave

**anus, -ūs** (f.) an old woman

**anxius, -a, -um** anxious, worried, troubled

**Āonius, -a, -um** of Aonia, Boeotian; of or connected with the Muses, poetic

**aperiō, -īre, -uī, -tum** to reveal, disclose

**apex, apicis** (m.) a tip of a flame

**apis, -is** (f.) bee

**Apollineus, -a, -um** of or pertaining to Apollo

**aptō, -āre, -āvī, -ātum** to fit, put into position

**aptus, -a, -um** (+ dat.) appropriate, fitting, suited

**~aqua, -ae** (f.) water, sea

**aquila, -ae** (f.) eagle

**aquōsus, -a, -um** watery, wet

**āra, -ae** (f.) altar

**arātor, -ōris** (m.) ploughman

**aratrum, -ī** (n.) plow

**~arbor, -oris** (f.) tree

**arboreus, -a, -um** of or pertaining to trees, arboreal

**arcus, -ūs** (m.) bow

**ardeō, -ēre, arsī, arsum** to burn, be inflamed

**arduum, -ī** (n.) high elevation

**arduus, -a, -um** tall, lofty

**ārea, -ae** (f.) open space out-of-doors

**argentum, -ī** (n.) silver

**argēus, -a, -um** Greek

**āridus, -a, -um** dry

**arista, -ae** (f.) harvest

**~arma, -ōrum** (n. pl.) arms, weapons; fighting, war

**armātus, -a, -um** armed

**armentum, -ī** (n.) herd

**~ars, -tis** (f.) skill, art

**artus, -ūs** (m.) limb of a tree or body; a joint of the body

**arvum, -ī** (n.) field, ploughed land; territory, country

**arx, -cis** (f.) summit, peak

**asper, -era, -erum** wild, rough, harsh

**aspiciō, -ere, -spexī, -spectum** to look at, gaze upon, observe

**~at** (conj.) at least, but, yet; while, whereas

**āter, ātra, ātrum** black, dark-colored, stained

**Atlantiadēs, -ae** (m.) Mercury, a grandson of Atlas

**~atque** (conj.) and in fact, and what is more, and indeed; and even

**Atrīdēs, -ae** (m.) a male descendant of Atreus, king of Argos and Mycenae; usually used of Agamemnon

attenuō, -āre, -āvī, -ātum to enfeeble, lessen, weaken

Atticus, -ī (m.) Atticus

attollō, -ere to lift up, raise

attonitus, -a, -um dazed, astounded

auctor, -ōris (m.) founder, author, originator

auctus, -a, -um increased in intensity

audax, -ācis bold, confident

audeō, -ēre, ausus to go so far as to, dare, have the courage

audiō, -īre, -īvī, -ītum to hear

auferō, -ferre, abstulī, ablātum to carry away, carry off

augeō, -ēre, auxī, auctum to increase, augment, strengthen

Augustus, -ī (m.) Caesar Augustus, emperor

Augustus, -a, -um of or pertaining to the emperor Augustus

~aura, -ae (f.) breeze, air

aurātus, -a, -um golden

aureus, -a, -um golden

auris, -is (f.) ear

Aurōra, -ae (f.) Aurora, goddess of the dawn

aurum, -ī (n.) gold

auspicium, -ī (n.) portent, fortune, luck

~aut (conj) or

aut . . . aut either . . . or

autumnālis, -e autumnal

avārus, -a, -um greedy, avaricious, miserly

~avēna, -ae (f.) stem, stalk

āversor, -ārī, -ātus to turn away from in disgust, reject

avis, avis (f.) bird

āvius, -a, -um distant, remote

## B

Babylōnius, -a, -um Babylonian

bāca, -ae (f.) olive; pearl

baculum, -ī (n.) walking stick, staff

Baucis, -idis (f.) Baucis, wife of Philemon

~bellum, -ī (n.) war

bellus, -a, -um pretty, beautiful

bene (adv.) well

bicolor, -ōris having two colors

bicornis, -e having two prongs

blanditia, -ae (f.) flattery, compliment, endearing comment

blandus, -a, -um charming, seductive, caressing

bonus, -a, -um good, worthy, reliable

Boōtēs, -ae (m.) Bootes, a constellation

bōs, bovis (m., f.) bull, cow

brācchium, -ī (n.) arm

brevis, -e short

Brīsēis, -idos (f.) Briseis, Achilles' slave and concubine

būbō, -ōnis (m.) the horned owl

bustum, -ī (n.) tomb

buxus, -ī (f.) boxwood

## C

cacūmen, -cūminis (n.) the tip or top of a tree

cadō, -ere, cecidī, cāsum to fall down

cādūcifer, -erī (m.) Mercury, the bearer of the caduceus

caedēs, -is (f.) slaughter, killing

caedō, -ere, cecīdī, caesum to kill, murder, slaughter

caelebs, -libis unmarried male, bachelor

caelicola, -ae (m., f.) an inhabitant of heaven

caelō, -āre, -āvī, -ātum to engrave, emboss

caelum, -ī (n.) sky, heaven

caeruleus, -a, -um blue, greenish blue

caleō, -ēre, -uī to be hot or warm

callidus, -a, -um clever, resourceful

Calymnē, -ēs (f.) an island off the coast of Asia Minor

campus, -ī (m.) field

candidus, -a, -um glistening

canis, canis (m.) dog, hound

canistrum, -ī (n.) a basket

canna, -ae (f.) a small reed

canō, -ere, cecinī, cantum to sing, tell of, relate

cantō, -āre, -āvī, -ātum to sing, celebrate in song

capillus, -ī (m.) hair

capiō, -ere, cēpī, captum to capture, contain

Capitōlium, -ī (n.) the Capitoline Hill

captīvus, -a, -um captured, hunted

captō, -āre, -āvī, -ātum to seek out; try to catch

captus, -a, -um captured

caput, -itis (n.) head

cardō, -inis (m.) hinge

careō, -ēre, -uī, -itum (+ abl.) to be lacking

cāricus, -a, -um carian, a type of fig

cariōsus, -a, -um decayed, withered

~carmen, -minis (n.) poetry, song

carnifex, -ficis (m.) executioner

carpō, -ere, -sī, -tum to pass over, pursue one's way

cārus, -a, -um beloved, dear

casa, -ae (f.) cottage

castra, -ōrum (n. pl.) camp

cāsus, -ūs (m.) misfortune, event

caterva, -ae (f.) band, squadron, troop

Catullus, -ī (m.) Catullus

causa, -ae (f.) cause, reason, inspiration

causor, -ārī, -ātus to plead as an excuse or reason

cautus, -a, -um cautious

cavus, -a, -um hollow, concave

cēdō, -ere, cessī, cessum to yield, give way; to be inferior

celeber, -bris, -bre crowded, populous, festive

celer, -eris, -ere swift

celsus, -a, -um high, lofty

~cēra, -ae (f.) wax, beeswax

Cerēs, -eris (f.) Ceres, goddess of open fields and agriculture

certē (adv.) at any rate, at least; certainly, without a doubt

~certus, -a, -um accurate, precise, sure

cerva, -ae (f.) deer

cervix, -īcis (f.) neck

cēterus, -a, -um the rest of, remaining

cicūta, -ae (f.) poisonous hemlock (*conium maculatum*)

cingō, -ere, cinxī, cinctum to gird, encircle, surround, bind

cinis, -eris (m.) ashes, embers

circumdō, -are, -edī, -atum (+ abl.) to surround, encircle

cithara, -ae (f.) lyre

citus, -a, -um rapid, speedy

clāmō, -āre, -āvī, -ātum to shout

Claros, -ī (f.) Claros, a small town, sacred to Apollo, on the central coast of Asia Minor

clārus, -a, -um loud, shrill

claudō, -ere, -sī, -sum to close, shut

clāvus, -ī (m.) nail

clīvus, -ī (m.) slope, incline

coactus, -a, -um curdled

coctilis, -e of baked bricks

coeō, -īre, -iī, -itum to come together, unite

coepī, coepisse, coeptum to begin

coerceō, -ēre, -uī, -itum to restrain, restrict, control, bind up

cognitor, -ōris (m.) attorney

cognitus, -a, -um known to be

cognoscō, -ere, -nōvī, -nitum to recognize

cōgō, -ere, coēgī, coactum to force, compel; to bring together

colligō, -ere, -lēgī, -lectum to gather together, collect

collis, -is (m.) hill, mountain

collum, -ī (n.) neck

colō, -ere, -uī, cultum to till, cultivate; to worship

~color, -ōris (m.) color

columba, -ae (f.) dove

columna, -ae (f.) column, pillar

coma, -ae (f.) hair

comes, -itis (m., f.) companion

comitō, -āre, -āvī, -ātum to follow

commendō, -āre, -āvī, -ātum to recommend, make agreeable or attractive

committō, -ere, -mīsī, -missum to entrust

commūnis, -e shared, common

cōmō, -ere, -psī, -ptum to adorn, arrange

complector, -ī, -plexus to embrace

complexus, -ūs (m.) embrace

compōnō, -ere, -posuī, -positum to compose, put together

comprimō, -ere, -pressī, -pressum to pack closely or densely, squeeze

comptus, -a, -um adorned

concha, -ae (f.) shell

concidō, -ere, -ī to fall, collapse

concipiō, -ere, -cēpī, -ceptum to produce, form; to conceive

concordō, -āre, -āvī, -ātum to agree, harmonize

concors, -cordis agreeing, harmonious

concutiō, -ere, -cussī, -cussum to shake

conditus, -a, -um preserved

condō, -ere, -idī, -itum to inter, lay to rest

confugiō, -ere, -fūgī to flee to for safety

congestus, -a, -um piled up

coniugium, -ī (n.) marriage

coniunx, -iugis (f.) wife, bride; husband

conligō, -ere, -lēgī, -lectum to gather together, collect

conlocō, -āre, -āvī, -ātum to place, position, arrange

conpescō, -ere, -uī to quench

conplector, -ī, -plexus to embrace

conpōnō, -ere, -posuī, -positum to place together

conprendō, -ere, -dī, -sum to seize, catch hold of

conscius, -ī (m.) accomplice, conspirator

consenescō, -ere, -senuī to grow old

consors, -rtis (f.) partner

conspiciō, -ere, -spexī, -spectum to see, witness

constō, -āre, -stitī to take up a position; to stand up

consuescō, -ere, -suēvī, -suētum to be in the habit of, become accustomed to

consūmō, -ere, -psī, -ptum to consume, devour

contentus, -a, -um content, satisfied

conterminus, -a, -um nearby, adjacent

contiguus, -a, -um adjacent, neighboring

contingō, -ere, -tigī, -tactum to come about, happen

continuō (adv.) forthwith, immediately, without delay

contrā (+ acc.) on the opposite side; (adv.) to the opposite side

cōnūbium, -ī (n.) the rite of marriage

conveniens, -entis (+ dat.) fitting, appropriate, consistent

conveniō, -īre, -vēnī, -ventum to be suitable or adapted for; to come together, meet

convincō, -ere, -vīcī, -victum to prove, demonstrate

Corinna, -ae (f.) Corinna

corniger, -era, -erum having horns

cornū, -ūs (n.) horn, bow

cornum, -ī (n.) a cornelian cherry

~corpus, -oris (n.) body

Corsicus, -a, -um of or belonging to the island of Corsica off the western coast of Italy

cortex, -icis (m.) outer bark of a tree

crātēr, -ēris (m.) a mixing bowl for wine

crēdibilis, -e capable of being believed, credible, likely

crēdō, -ere, -idī, -itum to believe, trust

crescō, -ere, crēvī, crētum to grow, increase; arise

Crētē, -ēs (f.) the island of Crete

crīmen, -minis (n.) reproach, blame; evil thing

crīnis, crīnis (m.) hair, tresses

cruentō, -āre, -āvī, -ātum to stain with blood

cruentus, -a, -um bloody

cruor, -ōris (m.) blood; bloodshed; gore

crūs, crūris (n.) lower leg, shin

crux, crucis (f.) wooden frame or cross on which criminals were hanged or impaled

cultus, -a, -um refined, sophisticated, elegant, revered

~cum (conj.) when; (prep. + abl.) with, along with

cunctus, -a, -um all; every

cupīdō, -dinis (f.) desire, longing

Cupīdō, -dinis (m.) Cupid

cupiō, -ere, -īvī, -ītum to desire

cur (adv.) why?

cūra, -ae (f.) care, anxiety, worry; object of concern, beloved person

cūrō, -āre, -āvī, -ātum to bother with, care about

currō, -ere, cucurrī, cursum to run, fly quickly

cursus, -ūs (m.) running, rushing

curvāmen, -minis (n.) curvature, arc

cuspis, -pidis (f.) spear, lance; sharp point, tip

custōdia, -ae (f.) defence, guard

custōs, -ōdis (m., f.) watchman, doorkeeper

Cyprus, -ī (f.) the island of Cyprus

Cytherēa, -ae (f.) Venus

# D

Daedalus, -ī (m.) Daedalus, builder of the labyrinth in Crete and father of Icarus

damnōsus, -a, -um ruinous, destructive,

Daphnē, -ēs (f.) Daphne, daughter of the river god Peneus; loved by Apollo and changed into a laurel tree

daps, dapis (f.) feast, meal

dē (+ abl.) from

dea, -ae (f.) goddess

debeō, -ēre, -uī, -itum to owe, be indebted to

decens, -entis graceful, attractive

decet, -ēre, -uit to be right, fitting, proper; to be becoming or appropriate

decor, -ōris (m.) beauty, good looks
dēdecet, -ēre, -uit to disgrace, dishonor
dēdicō, -āre, -āvī, -ātum to dedicate
dēferō, -ferre, -tulī, -lātum to bring down, carry down
dēfleō, -ēre, -ēvī, -ētum to lament, feel sorrow
dēlicia, -ae (f.) pleasure, delight
Dēlius, -iī (m.) Apollo
Dēlos, -ī (f.) Delos, an island in the Aegean
Delphicus, -a, -um of or connected to Delphi
dēlūbrum, -ī (n.) temple, shrine
dēmissus, -a, -um low, close to the ground
dēmittō, -ere, -mīsī, -missum to thrust, drive
dēmō, -ere, -psī, -ptum to remove, take away
densus, -a, -um thick, dense
dēpōnō, -ere, -posuī, -positum to lay aside, get rid of; to allay
dēprendō, -ere, -ī, -prensum to catch, discover
dēserō, -ere, -uī, -tum to withdraw, desert, abandon
dēserviō, -īre to serve zealously, devote oneself
dēsīdia, -ae (f.) idleness, inactivity, leisure
dēsidiōsus, -a, -um idle, lazy
dēsinō, -ere, -si(v)ī, -situm to cease, stop, desist
dēsultor, -ōris (m.) a circus rider who leaps from horse to horse
~deus, -ī (m.) god, deity
dēvoveō, -ēre, -vōvī, -vōtum to curse
dexter, -tra, -trum right, righthand
Diāna, -ae (f.) Diana, twin sister to Apollo, virgin goddess of woodlands
~dīcō, -ere, dixī, dictum to say; to appoint, fix
diēs, -ēī (f.) day
difficilis, -e troublesome
~digitus, -ī (m.) finger; toe
dignus, -a, -um worthy
dīmittō, -ere, -mīsī, -missum to direct oneself to; to let go
dīmoveō, -ēre, -mōvī, -mōtum to move about
dīrus, -a, -um dreadful, awful
discēdō, -ere, -cessī, -cessum to depart, go away
discinctus, -a, -um easygoing, undisciplined
discrīmen, -inis (n.) difference, distinction
dispār, -ris unequal, dissimilar
diū (adv.) for a long time

dīvellō, -ere, -vulsī, -vulsum to tear apart, tear open, tear in two
dīversus, -a, -um differing, distinct
~dō, dare, dedī, datum to give; to allow, cause to go
doctus, -a, -um expert, skilled
dolens, -entis grieving, sorrowing
dolor, -ōris (m.) pain, grief
domina, -ae (f.) mistress
dominus, -ī (m.) master, owner
domō, -āre, -āvī, -ātum to boil soft
domus, -ī (f.) house, home, household
dōnec (conj.) as long as
dōnō, -āre, -āvī, -ātum to give as a gift, grant
dubitō, -āre, -āvī, -ātum to hesitate; to doubt
dubius, -a, -um uncertain
dūcō, -ere, dūxī, ductum to lead; to shape, develop, mold
~dum (conj.) while
duo, -ae, -o two
duplex, -plicis twofold, deceitful, duplicitous
duplicō, -āre, -āvī, -ātum to double in size or amount
dūrus, -a, -um stubborn, hard; unsympathetic, uncaring, dull
~dux, -cis (m.) general, leader

# E

~ē, ex (+ abl.) from
~ebur, -oris (n.) ivory
eburneus, -a, -um of ivory
eburnus, -a, -um of ivory
ecce (interj.) behold! look!
ēdō, -ere, -idī, -itum to publish; produce, put forth; to deliver a message, utter
efficiō, -ere, -fēcī, -fectum to cause to be, become
effūsus, -a, -um loose, flowing
~ego I
ēgredior, -ī, -gressus to go out, leave
ei (interj.) oh!
ēiaculor, -ārī, -ātus to shoot forth
elegī, -ōrum (m. pl.) elegiac verses
ēlīdō, -ere, -lisī, -lisum to expel, force out, drive out
ēlūdō, -ere, -lūsī, -lūsum to elude, avoid capture
ēmicō, -āre, -āvī, -ātum to spurt, shoot forth

**ēmodulor, -ārī, -ātum** to sing in rhythm
**enim** (conj.) indeed, truly
**ensis, -is** (m.) sword
**~eō, īre, i(v)ī, itum** to go
**eōdem** (adv.) to the same place
**ephēmeris, -idos** (f.) a record book, daybook, diary
**epulae, -ārum** (f. pl.) feast, banquet
**eques, -itis** (m.) a member of the equestrian order
**equidem** (adv.) truly, indeed
**equus, -ī** (m.) horse
**ergo** (adv.) therefore, for that reason
**ērigō, -ere, -rexī, -rectum** to raise oneself
**eripiō, -ere, -ripuī, -reptum** to snatch, pluck
**errō, -āre, -āvī, -ātum** to wander about
**ērubescō, -ere, -buī** to blush with shame or modesty
**ērudiō, -īre, -īvī, -ītum** to teach, instruct
**~et** (conj.) and; also; even
**et ... et** both ... and
**etiam** (adv.) even; likewise; indeed
**etsī** (conj.) even if, although
**Eurus, -ī** (m.) Eurus, the east wind
**exaudiō, -īre, -īvī, -ītum** to hear, listen
**excēdō, -ere, -cessī, -cessum** to go away, pass out of, depart
**excipiō, -ere, -cēpī, -ceptum** to accept, receive
**exeō, -īre, -iī, -itum** to go out; emerge
**exhorreō, -ēre** to shudder
**exiguus, -a, -um** small, slight
**exilium, -ī** (n.) exile
**eximō, -ere, -ēmī, -emptum** to take away, banish
**exitium, -ī** (n.) destruction, ruin
**exōsus, -a, -um** hating, despising
**expallescō, -ere, -paluī** to turn pale
**experiens, -ntis** active
**expers, -pertis** (+ gen.) lacking experience or knowledge, free from
**extendō, -ere, -dī, -tum** to stretch out, thrust out
**exterō, -ere, -trīvī, -trītum** to wear down, trample on
**exterreō, -ēre, -uī, -itum** to terrify, frighten
**extinguō, -ere, -tinxī, -tinctum** to die, perish
**extrēmus, -a -um** farthest, outermost
**exuviae, -ārum** (f. pl.) spoils

# F

**fabricō, -āre, -āvī, -ātum** to work, fashion, shape
**fabrīlis, -e** of or belonging to a metalworker, skilled; fabricated
**fābula, -ae** (f.) gossip, scandal, myth, story
**faciēs, -iēī** (f.) appearance, looks, shape; beauty
**~faciō, -ere, fēcī, factum** to make, do; to bring about, inspire; to act; to reveal, to see that
**faex, -cis** (f.) the dregs or sediment of any liquid, particularly of wine; brine
**fāgineus, -a, -um** of the beech tree
**fāgus, -ī** (f.) beech tree
**~fallō, -ere, fefellī, falsum** to deceive, trick; to fail; to while away, beguile
**falsus, -a, -um** false, not genuine
**fama, -ae** (f.) reputation
**famulus, -ī** (m.) servant, attendant
**fateor, -ērī, fassus** to profess, agree; acknowledge
**fatīgō, -āre, -āvī, -ātum** to exhaust, tire out
**fātum, -ī** (n.) destiny, death, end
**favilla, -ae** (f.) ashes of a fire
**favus, -ī** (m.) honeycomb
**fax, facis** (f.) torch, firebrand
**fēcundus, -a, -um** fertile, fruitful
**fēlīciter** (adv.) successfully
**fēlix, -īcis** fruitful, fertile
**fēmina, -ae** (f.) woman
**fēmineus, -a, -um** female, feminine, womanly
**fera, -ae** (f.) wild animal
**~ferō, ferre, tulī, lātum** to tell, relate; to carry, bear, bring
**ferreus, -a, -um** iron-like, hardhearted, unfeeling
**ferrum, -ī** (n.) iron, steel; blade, sword
**~ferus, -a, -um** fierce, wild
**fervens, -ntis** hot, fresh; boiling, bubbling
**festum, -ī** (n.) holiday, festival
**festus, -a, -um** (+ diēs) holiday
**fētus, -ūs** (m.) fruit or product of a plant
**fictilis, -e** earthenware, pottery
**fidēs, -ēī** (f.) good faith, honesty, honor
**fīdus, -a, -um** faithful, loyal
**fīgō, -ere, -xī, -xum** to pierce, run through; to fix, fasten, lodge
**figūra, -ae** (f.) shape, appearance

fīlia, -ae (f.) daughter
fīlius, -ī (m.) son
fīlum, -ī (n.) yarn, thread
findō, -ere, fidī, fissum to split
fīniō, -īre, -īvī, -ītum to finish, end
fīnis, fīnis (m.) boundary, remotest limit
fīō, fierī to become, be made
fistula, -ae (f.) pipe, tube; pan-pipe
flāmen, -minis (n.) wind, breeze
flamma, -ae (f.) flame
flāvens, -entis yellow, golden
flāvescō, -ere to become golden
flāvus, -a, -um fair-haired, blonde; yellow
flectō, -ere, flexī, flectum to bend
fleō, -ēre, -ēvī, -ētum to weep, weep for
flētus, -ūs (m.) weeping, tears
flōs, -ōris (m.) flower, blossom
flūmen, -minis (n.) river
flūmineus, -a, -um of or associated with a river
focus, -ī (m.) hearth, fireplace
folium, -ī (n.) leaf of a plant
fons, -ntis (m.) spring of water
forāmen, -minis (n.) hole, aperture
forās (adv.) out-of-doors
foris, foris (f.) door, double door
forma, -ae (f.) appearance; good looks, beauty
formōsus, -a, -um beautiful
fors, -tis (f.) chance, luck
forte (adv.) by chance, accidentally
fortis, -e strong, courageous, brave, powerful
fortiter (adv.) vigorously, powerfully, with great force
foveō, -ēre, fōvī, fōtum to make warm
frangō, -ere, frēgī, fractum to break, smash
fretum, -ī (n.) strait, sea
frīgus, -oris (n.) cold, chill
frondeō, -ēre to grow foliage
frons, -dis (f.) foliage, leafy boughs
frons, -tis (f.) forehead, brow
fruor, -ī, -ctus to enjoy
frutex, -icis (f.) green growth
fuga, -ae (f.) flight, fleeing
fugax, -ācis running away, fleeing
~fugiō, -ere, -ī, -itum to flee

fugō, -āre, -āvī, -ātum to cause to flee, drive away, repel
fulgeō, -ēre, fulsī to glisten, gleam
fulica, -ae (f.) waterfowl, coot
fūmō, -āre, -āvī, -ātum to give off smoke
funēbris, -e deadly, funereal
fungor, -ī, functus to perform, observe
furca, -ae (f.) a length of wood with a forked end
furtīvus, -a, -um clandestine, secret

# G

galea, -ae (f.) helmet
Gallicus, -a, -um of Gaul
garrulus, -a, -um loquacious, talkative, wordy
gaudeō, -ēre, gāvīsus to rejoice; to be pleased
gelidus, -a, -um icy cold
geminus, -a, -um double; pair of, twin
gemma, -ae (f.) jewel, gem
gena, -ae (f.) cheek
gener, -erī (m.) son-in-law
genialis, -e creative, festive
genitor, -ōris (m.) father; ancestor
gens, -tis (f.) race, group of people
genu, -ūs (n.) knee
gerō, -ere, gessī, gestum to wage; to bear, carry
gestāmen, -minis (n.) load, burden
gestiō, -īre, -īvī to desire eagerly, want, be anxious to
gignō, -ere, genuī, genitum to give birth to
gloria, -ae (f.) glory
gradus, -ūs (m.) step
graphium, -ī (n.) stylus
grātēs, -ium (f. pl.) thanks
grātus, -a, -um welcome; pleasant, attractive
gravis, grave heavy, weighty; important; hard to capture
gravō, -āre, -āvī, -ātum to make heavy, weigh down
grex, gregis (m.) flock

# H

~habeō, -ēre, -uī, -itum to have, possess; to hold
habilis, -e suitable, fit
habitābilis, -e inhabitable

habitō, -āre, -āvī, -ātum to live, dwell

hāc (adv.) on this side

hāc facio to be on a side

haereō, -ēre, haesī, haesum to cling; to be brought to a standstill; to be perplexed, hesitate

harundō, -dinis (f.) reed; shaft of an arrow, arrow

haud (adv.) not

hauriō, -īre, hausī, haustum to swallow up, consume; to drink in, draw in

haustus, -ūs (m.) a drawn quantity of liquid, drink

Hector, -oris (m.) Hector, son of Priam, prince of Troy

Hēliades, -um (f. pl.) daughters of the sun god Helios

Helicē, -ēs (f.) the constellation Ursa Major

Helicōnius, -a, -um of Helicon

herba, -ae (f.) plant, herb

hērēs, -ēdis (m.) heir, successor

hērōs, -ōos (m.) hero

hesternus, -a, -um yesterday's

heu (interj.) alas

~hic, haec, hoc this, the latter

hīc (adv.) here, in this place

hinc (adv.) from this place; on this side

hodiē (adv.) today

holus, -eris (n.) vegetable (i.e., cabbage, turnip)

honestus, -a, -um honorable

honor, -ōris (m.) honor, mark of esteem, glory

hōra, -ae (f.) hour, time

horridus, -a, -um rough in manners, rude, uncouth; hairy

hortor, -ārī, -ātus to encourage

hortus, -ī (m.) garden

hospes, -itis (m.) visitor, stranger, guest; (adj.) of or pertaining to a guest

~hostis, -is (m.) enemy

hūc (adv.) here, to this place

humilis, -e humble, lowly

humus, -ī (f.) earth, ground

Hymēn (m.) the god of marriage, wedding

Hymettius, -a, -um of or pertaining to Mt. Hymettus near Athens, famous for its honey

# I

~iaceō, -ēre, -uī, -tum to lie down, lie; to be overthrown

~iam (adv.) now

ibi (adv.) there, in that place

Īcarus, -ī (m.) Daedalus's son

iciō, -ere, īcī, ictum to strike, beat

ictus, -ūs (m.) blow, stroke, thrust

īdem, eadem, idem the same

ideō (adv.) for that reason

ignārus, -a, -um unaware, ignorant, unfamiliar, unknown, blind

ignāvus, -a, -um lazy, sluggish

~ignis, -is (m.) fire, star

ignōtus, -a, -um unfamiliar, unknown

īlia, -ium (n. pl.) the gut, groin

illāc (adv.) by that way

~ille, illa, illud that, the former; he, she

illīc (adv.) there, in that place

illinc (adv.) on the other side

imbellis, -e not suited to warfare, unwarlike

imber, -bris (m.) rain

imitor, -ārī, -ātus to imitate, resemble

immundus, -a, -um unclean, foul, impure

impediō, -īre, -īvī, -ītum to hinder, impede

impellō, -ere, -pulī, -pulsum to push forward, urge on

īmus, -a, -um the lowest, bottommost

~in (+ acc.) over, affecting; for, towards; into; among; (+ abl.) in, on

incertus, -a, -um disarranged, not fixed; not sure, uncertain

incola, -ae (m., f.) inhabitant

increpō, -āre, -uī, -itum to make a loud rattle, clang, noise

incubō, -āre, -uī, -itum to throw oneself upon

incumbō, -ere, -cubuī to lean over or on; to lie on

inde (adv.) therefore, and so

indignor, -ārī, -ātum to consider as unworthy or improper

indignus, -a, -um not deserving, unworthy

indūcō, -ere, -dūxī, -ductum to cover, spread on or over

indūrescō, -escere, -uī to harden, become hard

inermis, -e unarmed, defenseless

iners, -rtis lazy, feeble

infāmis, -e infamous, disgraced

infēlix, -icis unhappy, ill-fated, unlucky

inferior, -ius lower, bottom, second

infestus, -a, -um hostile

ingeniōsus, -a, -um clever

ingenium, -ī (n.) character, spirit, nature

ingrātus, -a, -um ungrateful, thankless

inhaereō, -ēre, -haesī, -haesum to stick, cling, attach, grasp

inhibeō, -ēre, -uī, -itum to restrain, check, stop

inīquus, -a, -um resentful, discontented

inlinō, -ere, -lēvī, -litum to smear, coat

inmensus, -a, -um boundless, immense, huge

inmineō, -ēre to be poised over

inmūnis, -e (+ gen.) free from, exempt

innītor, -ī, -nixus to lean on, rest on

innumerus, -a, -um countless, innumerable,

innuptus, -a, -um unmarried

inornātus, -a, -um not adorned, dishevelled, unarranged

inpār, -ris unequal

inpatiens, -ntis impatient

inpediō, -īre, -īvī, -ītum to hinder, impede

inpellō, -ere, -pulī, -pulsum to push, drive, set in motion

inperfectus, -a, -um unfinished, incomplete

inpiger, -gra, -grum quick, energetic, tireless

inpius, -a, -um impious, irreverent, undutiful

inpleō, -ēre, -ēvī, -ētum to fill up

inpōnō, -ere, -posuī, -positum to place on

inpulsus, -ūs (m.) thrust, blow

~inquam, inquit to say

inquīrō, -ere, -quīsīvī, -sītus to inquire, ask

inrītō, -āre, -āvī, -ātum to provoke, arouse

insānus, -a, -um frenzied, mad, insane

insequor, -sequī, -secūtus to pursue

insīdō, -ere, -sēdī, -sessum to sink in, become embedded

insignis, -e outstanding, remarkable, distinguished

instar (n.) (+ gen.) according to, like

instruō, -ere, -xī, -ctum to instruct, equip, outfit

insula, -ae (f.) island

inter (+ acc.) among; between

intereā (adv.) meanwhile

intibum, -ı (n.) chicory or endive

intonsus, -a, -um unshorn, uncut

intrō, -āre, -āvī, -ātum to go into, enter

inūtilis, -e useless

invādō, -ere, -vāsī, -vāsum to attack, set on

inveniō, -īre, -ī, -tum to discover

inventum, -ī (n.) discovery, invention

invideō, -ēre, -vīdī, -vīsum to refuse, be unwilling

invidus, -a, -um envious, malevolent

Īō (f.) Io

~ipse, -a, -um oneself, itself

īra, -ae (f.) anger, rage, wrath

īrātus, -a, -um angry, furious

is, ea, id he, she, it; this, that

iste, -a, -ud that of yours

ita (adv.) thus, in this way

iter, -ineris (n.) journey, passage

iterum (adv.) again, another time

iubeō, -ēre, iussi, iussum to order, bid, command

iūdicium, -ī (n.) decision, pronouncement

iugālis, -e nuptial, matrimonial

iūgerum, -ī (n.) a measurement of land equal approximately to two-thirds of an acre

iugōsus, -a, -um hilly, mountainous

iungo, -ere, -xī, -ctum to join (in marriage)

Iūnōnius, -a, -um of or pertaining to Juno

Iuppiter, Iovis (m.) Jupiter

iūs, iūris (n.) authority, jurisdiction, power, right

iustus, -a, -um just, fair

iuvenālis, -e youthful

iuvenca, -ae (f.) heifer, cow

iuvencus, -ī (m.) young bull

iuvenis, -e young

# L

lābor, -ī, lāpsus to slip, slide; to drip

labor, -ōris (m.) labor, toil, hardship, task

labōrō, -āre, -āvī, -ātum to be anxious, worried, distressed

lac, -ctis (n.) milk

~lacertus, -ī (m.) upper arm

lacrima, -ae (f.) tear

laedō, -ere, laesī, laesum to harm, injure

laetus, -a, -um joyful

laevus, -a, -um left, lefthand

laniō, -āre, -āvī, -ātum to tear, mangle

lapillus, -ī (m.) small stone, gem

lascīvus, -a, -um naughty, unrestrained, mischievous

lassō, -āre, -āvī, -ātum to tire, exhaust

lātē (adv.) over a large area, widely

latebra, -ae (f.) hiding place

lateō, -ēre, -uī to hide; to take refuge; to be concealed, lie hidden

Latius, -a, -um Roman

lātus, -a, -um broad, wide

laudō, -āre, -āvī, -ātum to praise

laurea, -ae (f.) the laurel/bay tree

laurus, -ī (f.) foliage of the laurel (bay) tree; the laurel tree

laus, -dis (f.) praise, glory

lea, -ae (f.) lioness

leaena, -ae (f.) lioness

Lebinthos, -ī (f.) an island off the east coast of Greece

lectus, -ī (m.) bed, couch

~legō, -ere, lēgī, lectum to choose, select, pick out; to read

leō, -ōnis (m.) lion

lepus, -oris (m.) hare

lētum, -ī (n.) death

levis, -e light, not ponderous

leviter (adv.) lightly

levō, -āre, -āvī, -ātum to lift off, remove; to relieve, support

lex, lēgis (f.) law, rule; sine lege in disorder, unruly

liber, -brī (m.) inner bark of a tree

lībertās, -tātis (f.) liberty

lībrō, -āre, -āvī, -ātum to level, balance

licet, -ēre, -uī, -itum it is permitted, one may; (conj.) although

lignum, -ī (n.) wood, firewood

līlium, -ī (n.) lily

līmen, -minis (n.) threshold, doorstep

līmes, -mitis (m.) path, track

līnum, -ī (n.) thread, string

liquidus, -a, -um liquid, fluid

lītoreus, -a, -um of the seashore

littera, -ae (f.) letter

līvor, -ōris (m.) bluish coloring, bruise

~locus, -ī (m., n. pl.) place, open land

~longus, -a, -um long, tall

~loquor, -quī, -cūtus to speak

luctus, -ūs (m.) grief, mourning

lūdō, -ere, lūsi, lūsum to trick, deceive

lūmen, -minis (n.) light, brilliance; eye

lūna, -ae (f.) moon

lūnāris, -e of or pertaining to the moon

lūnō, -āre, -āvī, -ātum to curve, bend

luō, -ere, -ī to pay as a penalty, amend for

lupus, -ī (m.) wolf

lustrō, -āre, -āvī, -ātum to move through or around, roam

lūsus, -ūs (m.) playing, sporting

lux, lūcis (f.) light of day; sub luce at dawn

Lyaeus, -ī (m.) Bacchus

lyra, -ae (f.) lyre, lute

# M

mactō, -āre, -āvī, -ātum to kill, slay, sacrifice

madefaciō, -ere, -fēcī, -factum to soak, drench

madeō, -ēre, -uī to grow wet

Maenas, -adis (f.) female worshipper of Bacchus, Bacchante, Maenad

magis (adv.) more

~magnus, -a, -um great, large

maior, -ius greater, larger

malum, -ī (n.) evil, wickedness

mālum, -ī (n.) an apple

malus, -a, -um wicked

mandō, -āre, -āvī, -ātum to order, command

māne (adv.) early in the day, morning

maneō, -ēre, -sī, -sum to remain, stay

Mantua, -ae (f.) the city of Mantua in the north of Italy

~manus, -ūs (f.) hand; armed force, band

margō, -inis (m.) margin

marītus, -ī (m.) husband

marmor, -oris (n.) marble

Mars, -tis (m.) Mars, god of war

massa, -ae (f.) heap, lump, mass

māter, -tris (f.) mother

māteria, -ae (f.) material, subject-matter

māteriēs, -iēī (f.) material, subject-matter

mātūrus, -a, -um mature, experienced

medicīna, -ae (f.) medicine

medicō, -āre, -āvī, -ātum to dye

medium, -ī (n.) a neutral or undecided state

~medius, -a, -um middle, middle of; between; in half, half, medium, moderate

medulla, -ae (f.) marrow

mel, mellis (n.) honey

melior, -ius better, finer, superior

melius (adv.) better, more fittingly

membrum, -ī (n.) part of the body; limb of tree or body

meminī, -isse to remember

mens, -tis (f.) mind; inclination

mensa, -ae (f.) table

menta, -ae (f.) mint

mereō, -ēre, -uī, -itum to earn

mergō, -ere, -rsī, -rsum to flood, inundate

mergus, -ī (m.) sea bird, gull

meritus, -a, -um deserving, just

mēta, -ae (f.) turning post, goal

metuō, -ere, -uī -ūtum to fear, be afraid

metus, -ūs (m.) fear

~meus, -a, -um my

micō, -āre, -āvī to flash, glitter, glisten

~mīles, -itis (m.) soldier

mīlitia, -ae (f.) military service

mīlitō, -āre, -āvī, -ātum to serve as a soldier, be a soldier

mille (n.) (indecl.) a thousand

Minerva, -ae (f.) Minerva, the goddess associated with handicrafts (particularly spinning) and war

minimus, -a, -um smallest, very small, least

ministerium, -ī (n.) duty, office, work

ministra, -ae (f.) an assistant

minium, -ī (n.) bright red dye, cinnabar

minor, -us smaller

Mīnōs, -ōis (m.) Minos, king of Crete

minuō, -ere, -uī, -ūtum to make smaller

minus (adv.) less, to a smaller degree

mīrābilis, -e wondrous, extraordinary

mīror, -ārī, -ātus to wonder at, be surprised

mīrus, -a, -um remarkable, extraordinary, wondrous

misceō, -ēre, -uī, mixtum to mix together, blend

~miser, -era, -erum wretched, miserable

miserābilis, -e pitiable

miserandus, -a, -um wretched, pitiable

~mittō, -ere, mīsī, missum to let go, set free; send, shoot

mixtus, -a, -um mixed

moderātē (adv.) gently, in a restrained manner

modicus, -a, -um moderate in size

~modo (adv.) just now, recently, lately; just, only

modus, -ī (m.) measure, meter, rhythm

moenia, -ium (n. pl.) defensive walls encircling a town

mollescō, -ere to become soft

molliō, -īre, -īvī, -ītum to soften, weaken

mollis, -e gentle, smooth; soft

moneō, -ēre, -uī, -itum to advise, recommend

monīle, -is (n.) necklace

monimentum, -ī (n.) memorial

monitus, -ūs (m.) warning, advising

mons, -tis (m.) mountain, mountainous country

mora, -ae (f.) delay

morior, -ī, mortuus to die

moror, -ārī, -ātus to delay, wait; to hold back

mors, -tis (f.) death

morsus, -ūs (m.) bite

mortālis, -e mortal, human

mōrum, -ī (n.) the fruit of the mulberry tree

mōrus, -ī (f.) mulberry tree

mōs, mōris (m.) character, morals, behavior

moveō, -ēre, mōvī, mōtum to move, strike; rouse

mox (adv.) soon

mucrō, -ōnis (m.) tip or point of a sword

multifidus, -a, -um split, splintered

multum (adv.) very, greatly

~multus, -a, -um much

mūnus, -eris (n.) gift, present; ritual duty

murmur, -is (n.) mutter, whisper

mūrus, -ī (m.) wall, city-wall

Mūsa, -ae (f.) Muse

mūtō, -āre, -āvī, -ātum to change, replace

mūtuus, -a, -um mutual, reciprocal

myrtus, -ī (f.) foliage of the myrtle tree

# N

nam (conj.) for, to be sure

Napē, -ēs (f.) Nape

narrō, -āre, -āvī, -ātum to tell, relate

nascor, -ī, nātus to be born

Nāsō, -ōnis (m.) Naso, Ovid's cognomen

nāta, -ae (f.) daughter

nātālis, -e of or belonging to birth

nātūra, -ae (f.) nature, natural world

~nātus, -ī (m.) son

nē (conj.) lest, in order that...not; do not

~nec and . . . not; not even

necō, -āre, -āvī, -ātum to kill, put to death

negō, -āre, -āvī, -ātum to say not; to deny

nempe (conj.) to be sure, no doubt, certainly

nemus, -oris (n.) wood, sacred grove

nepōs, -ōtis (m., f.) grandson, granddaughter

neque (conj.) and . . . not

nēquīquam (adv.) in vain

nervus, -ī (m.) string of a musical instrument or bow

nesciō, -īre, -īvī, -ītum not to know, to be unfamiliar with; nesciō quis some, little, insignificant

neu (conj.) nor

nēve (conj.) and that . . . not

nex, necis (f.) death

nīdus, -ī (m.) nest

niger, -gra, -grum black, dark-colored

nimbus, -ī (m.) cloudburst, rainstorm

nimis (adv.) too much, excessively, too

~nimium (adv.) excessively, extremely, very much

nimius, -a, -um too much, too great

Ninus, -ī (m.) Ninus, king of Assyria and second husband to Semiramis

nisi (conj.) if not

nītor, -tī, -sus to strive, move with difficulty, exert oneself

nitor, -ōris (m.) brilliance, brightness, splendor, elegance

niveus, -a, -um white, snowy-white

nix, nivis (f.) snow

nocens, -ntis guilty

nocturnus, -a, -um nightly, of the night

nolō, nolle, noluī, not to want or wish

~nōmen, -minis (n.) name, family name, fame, reputation

nōminō, -āre, -avī, -ātum to name, call by name

~nōn (adv.) not

nōndum (adv.) not yet

nōs we

noscō, -ere, nōvī, nōtum to learn

~noster, -tra, -trum our

nota, -ae (f.) note, mark

nōtitia, -ae (f.) acquaintance

notō, -āre, -āvī, -ātum to mark, inscribe, scratch; to notice

nōtus, -a, -um famous, well-known

novem (indecl.) nine

noviens (adv.) nine times

novissimus, -a, -um last, final

novitās, -tātis (f.) novelty, strange phenomenon

novō, -āre, -āvī, -ātum to make or devise as new

~novus, -a, -um new, unfamiliar

~nox, -ctis (f.) night

nūdō, -āre, -āvī, -ātum to make naked, expose

~nūdus, -a, -um bare, pure, open, simple; naked, unclothed

~nullus, -a, -um no one, nobody, nothing; no; insignificant, trifling

nūmen, -minis (n.) divine power, divinity

numerus, -ī (m.) number, rhythm, measure, meter

nunc (adv.) now, at this time

nūper (adv.) recently

nūtriō, -īre, -īvī, -ītum to encourage, foster

nūtus, -ūs (m.) nod

nux, -cis (f.) nut

nympha, -ae (f.) demi-goddess spirit of nature, nymph; unmarried girl

# O

**oblinō, -ere, -lēvī, -litum** to besmear, make dirty
**obscūrus, -a, -um** dim, dark
**obscēnus, -a, -um** polluted, foul, ill-omened
**obsequor, -sequī, -secūtus** to comply, gratify, humor
**observō, -āre, -āvī, -ātum** to watch over, guard
**obsideō, -ēre, -sēdī, -sessum** to occupy, beseige
**obstipescō, -ere, -stipuī** to be amazed, astonished
**obstō, -āre, -stitī, -stātum** to stand in the way, block the path
**obstruō, -ere, -xī, -ctum** to block, obstruct
**obtūsus, -a, -um** blunt, dull
**obvius, -a, -um** opposing, confronting
**occupō, -āre, -āvī, -ātum** to seize, occupy
**ōcior, ōcius** swifter, faster
**~oculus, -ī** (m.) eye
**ōdī, odisse, ōsum** to hate, dislike
**odōrātus, -a, -um** sweet-smelling, fragrant
**offensus, -a, -um** offended, displeased
**officium, -ī** (n.) duty
**ōlim** (adv.) a long time ago
**ōmen, -minis** (n.) omen
**~omnis, -e** each, every, all
**onus, -eris** (n.) burden
**opifer, -era, -erum** aid-bringing, helper
**opifex, -ficis** (m.) craftsman, artisan
**ops, opis** (f.) (sing.) aid, help, military strength; (pl.) wealth
**optō, -āre, -āvī, -ātum** to desire, wish for
**~opus, -eris** (n.) task, undertaking, work, job; need
**ōrāculum, -ī** (n.) oracular power, divine utterance
**orbis, -is** (m.) globe, world
**~ordō, -dinis** (m.) order; class, rank; a linear arrangement
**Oriens, -ntis** (m.) the East
**Ōrīōn, -ōnis** ( m.) the constellation Orion
**ornō, -āre, -āvī, -ātum** to adorn, decorate, attire
**ōrō, -āre, -āvī, -ātum** to pray, beseech, beg
**~ōs, ōris** (n.) face; mouth
**os, ossis** (n.) bone
**~osculum, -ī** (n.) mouth, lips; kiss
**ostendō, -ere, -tendī, -tentum** to show, point out
**ōtium, -ī** (n.) leisure
**ōvum, -ī** (n.) egg

# P

**paciscor, -ī, pactus** to agree upon
**pactum, -ī** (n.) agreement
**Paeān, -nis** (m.) Apollo, as healer; a hymn or praise addressed to Apollo
**Paelignus, -a, -um** of the Paelignian region in central Italy
**pāgina, -ae** (f.) page
**pallidus, -a, -um** pale, lacking color
**palma, -ae** (f.) fruit of the palm, a date
**palūs, -ūdis** (f.) swamp, floodwater
**paluster, -tris, -tre** marshy
**pandus, -a, -um** curved, bent, bowed
**Paphius, -a, -um** of or pertaining to the city of Paphos on Cyprus
**Paphos, -ī** (m.) the child of Pygmalion
**pār, paris** equal
**parātus, -ūs** (m.) preparation
**parcus, -a, -um** thrifty, frugal
**~pārens, -entis** (m., f.) ancestor, parent
**pāreō, -ēre, -uī, -itum** to obey
**pariēs, -etis** (m.) wall
**parilis, -e** similar, like
**pariter** (adv.) in the same manner, likewise; at the same time, simultaneously
**Parnāsus, -ī** (m.) Parnassus, a mountain in Greece at the base of which is Delphi, sacred to both Apollo and the Muses
**parō, -āre, -āvī, -ātum** to prepare
**Paros, -ī** (f.) Paros, an island in the Aegean Sea
**pars, -tis** (f.) part, portion; side
**parvus, -a, -um** small
**passus, -ūs** (m.) pace, stride
**pastor, -ōris** (m.) shepherd
**Patarēus, -a, -um** of or related to Patara, a coastal city in southern Asia Minor with an oracle of Apollo
**pateō, -ēre, -uī** to be visible or revealed; to be open
**~pater, -tris** (m.) father
**patior, -tī, passus** to allow, permit
**patrius, -a, -um** of or pertaining to a father
**patulus, -a, -um** broad
**paucus, -a, -um** few
**paulātim** (adv.) little by little, by degrees
**paulum** (adv.) a little bit, to a small extent

pauper, -eris poor, scanty

paupertās, -tātis (f.) poverty

paveō, -ēre to be frightened

~pectus, -oris (n.) chest, breast, heart

pelagus, -ī (n.) open sea

pellō, -ere, pepulī, pulsum to fend off, drive away, repel; to strike, beat

Pelopēius, -a, -um of or pertaining to the Peloponnesian peninsula

penātēs, -ium (n. pl.) the household gods

pendeō, -ēre, pependī to hang, hang down, fall

Pēnēis, -idos descended from the river god Peneus

Pēnēius, -a, -um of or connected with the river god Peneus

penitus (adv.) thoroughly, completely

~penna, -ae (f.) wing, feather

~per (+ acc.) through, throughout

peragō, -ere, -ēgī, -actum to carry out, perform

perārō, -āre, -āvī, -ātum to plow through, inscribe

percipiō, -ere, -cēpī, -ceptum to catch hold of

percutiō, -ere, -cussī, -cussum to strike, beat

~perdō, -ere, -idī, -itum to waste one's effort or time; to destroy

peremō, -ere, -ī, -ptum to kill

perennis, -e lasting, enduring

perferō, -ferre, -tulī, -lātum to suffer, endure, undergo; carry, convey

perīclum see perīculum

perīculum, -ī (n.) danger

perlegō, -ere, -lēgī, -lectum to read over, read through

permātūrescō, -ere, -tūruī to become fully ripe

perōdī, -disse, -sum to despise, loathe

perpetuus, -a, -um eternal, everlasting

persequor, -sequī, -secūtus to follow all the way, accompany

perveniō, -īre, -vēnī, -ventum to penetrate, extend, reach; to arrive

pervigilō, -āre, -āvī, -ātum to keep watch all night

~pēs, pedis (m.) foot; metrical foot

pestifer, -era, -erum deadly, pernicious, pestilential

~petō, -ere, -īvī, -ītum to seek, look for; to seek the hand of in marriage, to court

pharetra, -ae (f.) quiver

pharetrātus, -a, -um wearing a quiver

Philēmōn, -onis (m.) Philemon, husband of Baucis

Phoebē, -ēs (f.) Diana, twin sister to Apollo

Phoebus, -ī (m.) Apollo

Phrygia, -ae (f.) Phrygia, a region in central Asia Minor

pictus, -a, -um painted

Pīeridēs, -um (f. pl.) the Muses, daughters of Pierus

piger, -gra, -grum sluggish, inactive

pīla, -ae (f.) ball, sphere

piscis, -is (m.) fish

Pittheus, -eī (m.) Pittheus, son of Pelops and grandfather to Theseus

pius, -a, -um dutiful, conscientious, pious

~placeō, -ēre, -uī, -itum (+ dat.) to be pleasing or acceptable

placidus, -a, -um agreeable, kindly

plangor, -ōris (m.) beating, lamentation

plēnus, -a, -um full

plūma, -ae (f.) feather

plumbum, -ī (n.) lead

plūrimus, -a, -um most plentifully supplied, greatest in amount

plūs, plūris (n.) more

plūs (adv.) more

pōculum, -ī (n.) a drinking cup

poena, -ae (f.) penalty, punishment

poēta, -ae (m.) poet

pollex, -icis (m.) thumb

pompa, -ae (f.) ceremonial procession

pōmum, -ī (n.) fruit

~pōnō, -ere, posuī, positum to put, place, arrange; to lay aside, abandon

pontus, -ī (m.) sea

porta, -ae (f.) gate, entryway

poscō, -ere, poposcī to demand, ask for insistently

possideō, -ēre, -sēdī, -sessum to control

~possum, posse, potuī to be able

post (+ acc.) after

posterus, -a, -um next, following

postis, -is (m.) door jamb, door, lintel

postquam (conj.) after, when

potens, -tis powerful, mighty, influential

potentia, -ae (f.) power, influence

praebeō -ēre, -uī, -itum to offer, provide

praeceptum, -ī (n.) teaching, piece of advice

praecipitō, -āre, -āvī, -ātum to plunge down, sink

praecordia, -ōrum (n. pl.) heart, chest, breast

praeda, -ae (f.) prey

praedor, -ārī, -ātus to take as prey, catch

praeferō, -ferre, -tulī, -lātum (+ dat.) to prefer, esteem more

praeripiō, -ere, -ripuī, -reptum to seize, snatch away

praetereō, -īre, -iī, -itum to pass by

precor, -ārī, -ātus to pray for, implore, beg, beseech

premō, -ere, -ssī, -ssum to press on, push; to cover

prex, precis (f.) prayer

Priamēis, -idos (f.) Cassandra, daughter of Priam

prīmus, -a, -um first

prior, -us first, earlier

prius (adv.) first

prō (+ abl.) on account of, because of

proavus, -ī (m.) forefather

probō, -āre, -āvī, -ātum to authorize, sanction, approve

procul (adv.) far off, at a great distance

prōdūcō, -ere, -dūxī, -ductum to bring forth, lead forth

prohibeō, -ēre, -uī, -itum to prevent; to refuse

prōiciō, -ere, -iēcī, -iectum to throw down

prōlēs, -is (f.) offspring

prōmō, -ere, -psī, -ptum to bring forth, draw forth, produce

prōnus, -a, -um lying on the face or stomach, headlong

properō, -āre, -āvī, -ātum to hasten

Prōpoetides, -um (f. pl.) young women from Cyprus

prospiciō, -ere, -spexī, -spectum to see before one, have a view

prōsum, prōdesse, prōfuī, prōfutūrus to benefit, be helpful or useful to

prōtinus (adv.) forthwith, at once, immediately, suddenly

prōveniō, -īre, -vēnī, -ventum to come into being, arise

proximus, -a, -um next

pruīnōsus, -a, -um frosty

prūnum, -ī (n.) a plum

pudor, -ōris (m.) modesty

~puella, -ae (f.) girl, young woman

~puer, -ī (m.) boy

pulcher, -ra, -um beautiful

pullus, -a, -um dingy, somber

pulsō, -āre, -āvī, -ātum to beat, strike repeatedly

pulvis, -eris (m.) dust

purpureus, -a, -um radiant, glowing, blushing; purple, crimson

pūrus, -a, -um pure, unsoiled

putō, -āre, -āvī, -ātum to think, consider; to imagine

Pygmaliōn, -ōnis (m.) Pygmalion, king of Cyprus

Pyramus, -ī (m.) Pyramus

Pythōn, -ōnis (m.) a serpent slain by Apollo

# Q

quā (adv.) where, in which direction

quam (rel. adv.) than

quaerō, -ere, quaesīvī, -sītum to require, demand; to seek

quantō . . . tantō (adv.) by however much . . . by just so much

quantuluscumque, -acumque, -umcumque however small

quantus, -a, -um how great

quatiō, -ere, quassum to shake

-que and; -que . . . -que both . . . and . . .

quercus, -ūs (f.) oak tree; oak garland

queror, -rī, questus to complain

~quī, quae, quod who, which

quia (conj.) because, since

quīcumque, quaecumque, quodcumque the person who, whoever, whatever

quid (adv.) why? for what reason?

quidem (adv.) certainly, indeed, it is true

quinque five

~quis, quid who? what?

quisque, quaeque, quidque each, each one, each thing

quisquis, quidquid anyone who, whoever

quō (adv.) for that reason; in order that; by which degree, by how much

quod (conj.) because; that, the fact that

quondam (adv.) once, formerly

quoniam (conj.) since

~quoque (adv.) also, too

# R

**radius, -ī** (m.) ray of light

**rādix, -īcis** (f.) root; radish

**rādō, -ere, rāsī, -sum** to rub clean, erase; to graze, scrape, scratch

**rāmāle, -is** (n.) branches, twigs

**~rāmus, -ī** (m.) branch

**rapidus, -a, -um** swift-moving

**raucus, -a, -um** harsh-sounding, raucous

**recens, -ntis** recent, fresh

**recipiō, -ere, -cēpī, -ceptum** to receive, make welcome

**recondō, -ere, -idī, -itum** to close again

**reddō, -ere, -idī, -itum** to deliver; to give back, return

**redeō, -īre, -iī, -itum** to return

**redimīculum, -ī** (n.) band, wreath, garland

**redimiō, -īre, -iī, -ītum** to wreathe, encircle

**redoleō, -ēre** to give off a smell, be fragrant

**referō, -ferre, rettulī, relātum** to bring back, bring out

**rēfert, -ferre, -tulit** it is of importance

**refertus, -a, -um** crammed full

**refugiō, -ere, -fūgī** to shrink from, recoil from

**rēgia, -ae** (f.) royal palace, court

**regiō, -ōnis** (f.) direction

**regnō, -āre, -āvī, -ātum** to reign, govern, hold sway

**regnum, -ī** (n.) kingdom, domain

**relevō, -āre, -āvī, -ātum** to relieve, ease

**~relinquō, -ere, -liquī, -lictum** to leave behind

**remaneō, -ēre, -sī, -sum** to remain, stay put

**rēmigium, -ī** (n.) oars, wings

**remollescō, -ere** to grow soft again, melt

**remoror, -ārī, -ātus** to linger, delay

**removeō, -ēre, -mōvī, -mōtum** to remove

**renīdeō, -ēre** to smile with pleasure, beam

**renovō, -āre, -āvī, -ātum** to renew

**reperiō, -īre, repperī, repertum** to find, discover

**repertor, -ōris** (m.) originator, discoverer

**repetō, -ere, -īvī, -ītum** to repeat

**repleō, -ēre, -ēvī, -ētum** to refill, replenish

**repōnō, -ere, -posuī, -positum** to lay to rest

**repugnō, -āre, -āvī, -ātum** to resist, fight against

**requiēs, -ētis** (f.) (**requiem,** acc.) rest, relaxation

**requiescō, -ere, -quēvī, -quētum** to rest, lie at rest

**requīrō, -ere, -quīsīvī, -quīsītum** to ask, inquire about; to seek out, look for

**rēs, -eī** (f.) matter, thing

**rescribō, -ere, -scripsī, -scriptum** to write back in response

**resecō, -āre, -secuī, -sectum** to cut back, trim

**resīdō, -ere, -sēdī, -sessum** to fall back, subside

**resistō, -ere, -stitī** to halt, pause

**respiciō, -ere, -spexī, -spectum** to look back, look around

**respondeō, -ēre, -dī, -sum** to answer, reply

**restō, -āre, -itī** to linger, remain; to stand firm; to stop

**resupīnus, -a, -um** lying on one's back

**resurgō, -ere, -surrexī, -surrectum** to rise up again

**retractō, -āre, -āvī, -ātum** to handle or feel a second time

**retrō** (adv.) backwards

**revellō, -ere, -vellī, -vulsum** to remove, tear away

**reverentia, -ae** (f.) shyness, awe, modesty

**revocō, -āre, -āvī, -ātum** to summon back

**Rhēsus, -ī** (m.) Rhesus, a Thracian

**rictus, -ūs** (m.) open jaws

**rīdeō, -ēre, rīsī, rīsum** to laugh

**rigidus, -a, -um** rigid, stiff

**rigor, -ōris** (m.) stiffness, rigidity

**riguus, -a, -um** irrigated, well-watered

**rīma, -ae** (f.) crack

**rīvalis, -is** (m.) rival

**rōdō, -ere, rōsī, -sum** to eat away, erode

**rogō, -āre, -āvī, -ātum** to beg, implore

**rogus, -ī** (m.) funeral pyre

**Rōma, -ae** (f.) Rome

**rostrum, -ī** (n.) snout, muzzle

**rota, -ae** (f.) wheel

**rubeō, -ēre** to turn red

**rubor, -ōris** (m.) redness

**rudis, -e** crude, rough

**rūgōsus, -a, -um** wrinkled

**rumpō, -ere, rūpī, ruptum** to burst, break through

**rūpēs, -is** (f.) rocky cliff

**rursus** (adv.) in addition, besides

**rūs, rūris** (n.) countryside

**rusticus, -a, -um** rustic, crude, unrefined

# S

sacer, -cra, -crum sacred, holy

sacerdōs, -ōtis (m., f.) priest, priestess

saeculum, -ī (n.) generation

~saepe (adv.) often

saepēs, -is (f.) hedge

saevus, -a, -um wild, savage, untamed

sagitta, -ae (f.) arrow

sagittifer, -era, -erum loaded with arrows, arrow-bearing

salignus, -a, -um willow wood

saliō, -īre, -uī, -tum to jump, leap

salūs, -ūtis (f.) safety

Samos, -ī (f.) an island in the eastern Mediterranean Sea

sānābilis, -e curable

sanguis, -guinis (m.) blood, bloodline

sanguinulentus, -a, -um blood red

satis (adv.) enough

Sāturnius, -a, -um of Saturn, i.e., Jupiter

scelerātus, -a, -um wicked, accursed, impious

scindō, -ere, scicidī, scissum to split, rend, tear apart

sciō, -īre, -īvī, -ītum to know

scrībō, -ere, -psī, -ptum to write

sculpō, -ere, -psī, -ptum to carve

secō, -āre, -cuī, -ctum to cut

secundus, -a, -um second

~sed (conj.) but

sedeō, -ēre, sēdī, sessum to sit

sēdēs, -is (f.) house, dwelling

sedīle -is (n.) seat

sēducō, -ere, -dūxī, -ductum to move away, draw apart

sēdulus, -a, -um attentive, persistent, zealous

segnis, -e inactive, sluggish

semel (adv.) once, a single time

Semīramis, -idis (f.) Semiramis, a Syrian queen

~semper (adv.) always

senecta, -ae (f.) old age

senectūs, -ūtis (f.) old age

senex, senis old

senīlis, -e old, aged

senior, -ius older

~sentiō, -īre, sensī, sensum to feel, sense

sentis, -is (m.) bramble, briar

sepeliō, -īre, -īvī, sepultum to bury, entomb

sepulcrum, -ī (n.) tomb, grave

sequor, -quī, -cūtus to follow; to come next in order

sera, -ae (f.) a crossbar for locking a door

sermō, -ōnis (m.) talk, conversation

serpens, -entis (f., m.) snake, serpent

serta, -ōrum (n. pl.) garlands, wreaths

sērus, -a, -um late, after the expected time

servō, -āre, -āvī, -ātum to guard; save, keep

serviō, -īre, -īvī, -ītum to be devoted or subject to; to serve

sex six

~sī (conj.) if

~sīc (adv.) thus, in this way, in like manner

siccō, -āre, -āvī, -ātum to dry, dry up

siccus, -a, -um dry

Sīdonis, -idis of or pertaining to Sidon, a town on the Phoenician coast known for its puple dyeing process

sīdus, -eris (n.) constellation, star

signum, -ī (n.) signal, sign for action; military standard

silens, -entis silent

silex, -icis (m.) hard rock or stone; flint

silva, -ae (f.) forest, woodland

similis, -e like, similar

simplicitās, -tātis (f.) lack of sophistication, frankness

simul (adv.) together, with one another; at the same time

simulācrum, -ī (n.) image, statue

simulō, -āre, -āvī, -ātum to pretend, simulate

sincērus, -a, -um unblemished

sine (+ abl.) without

sinō, -ere, sīvī, situm to permit, allow to take place

sinuōsus, -a, -um having a bowed form, curved

sistō, -ere, stetī, statum to set, set down

sitis, -is (f.) thirst

situs, -ūs (m.) neglect, disuse

sōbrius, -a, -um sober, not intoxicated

socius, -a, -um of or pertaining to a partner, kindred, companionable, fellow

sōl, sōlis (m.) sun

soleō, -ēre, -itus to be accustomed to

solitus, -a, -um usual, accustomed

solum, -ī (n.) earth, soil

sōlus, -a, -um alone, only

solūtus, -a, -um loose, unfastened, undone; weak

somnus, -ī (m.) sleep, sleepiness

sōpītus, -a, -um sleepy

sopōrō, -āre, -āvī, -ātum to put to sleep

sordidus, -a, -um grimy, dirty, unwashed

soror, -ōris (f.) sister

spargō, -ere, sparsī, sparsum to scatter, strew

spatior, -ārī, -ātus to walk about

speciēs, -iēī (f.) appearance, impression

spectō, -āre, -āvī, -ātum to look at, observe

speculātor, -ōris (m.) scout, spy

spērō, -āre, -āvī, -ātum to hope for, look forward to; to expect

spēs, -eī (f.) hope, expectation

spīculum, -ī (n.) tip, point; arrow

splendidus, -a, -um bright, shining

sponda, -ae (f.) the frame of a bed or couch

spons, -ntis (f.) will, volition

spūmō, -āre, āvī, -ātum to foam, froth

stāgnum, -ī (n.) pool

statuō, -ere, -uī, -ūtum to make up one's mind, decide

sterilis, -e futile

sternō, -ere, strāvī, strātum to strew, lay low, spread over an area, throw down

stīpes, -itis (m.) tree trunk; woody branch

stipula, -ae (f.) stubble

stīva, -ae (f.) the shaft of a plow handle

stō, stāre, stetī, stātum to stand

strāmen, -inis (n.) straw thatch

strātum, -ī (n.) coverlet, throw

strēnuus, -a, -um restless, keen

strīdō, -ere, -ī to make a high-pitched sound; to whistle, shriek, hiss

stringō, -ere, -nxī, strictum to touch lightly, graze; to unsheath

strix, -igis (f.) a screech owl

stupeō, -ēre, -uī to be amazed, stunned, dazed

~sub (+ abl.) under, underneath; at the base of; (+ acc) at the base of, just at

subditus, -a, -um situated beneath

subeō, -īre, -īvī, -itum to spread upwards; to replace

sūbiciō, -ere, -iēcī, -iectum to harness, put under the control of

subscrībō, -ere, -scripsī, -scriptum to write below

subsīdō, -ere, -sēdī to give way

succintus, -a, -um having one's clothes bound up with a girdle or belt

succrescō, -ere, -ēvī to grow up as a replacement, to be supplied anew

sufferō, -ferre, sustulī, sublātum to hold up, sustain weight

suffundō, -ere, -fūdī, -fūsum to pour into, overspread; to color, redden, blush

suī himself, herself, itself, themselves

Sulmō, -ōnis (m.) Sulmo, in the province of Paelignia; the town of Ovid's birth

~sum, esse, fuī, futūrus to be

summittō, -ere, -mīsī, -missum to lower

summus, -a, -um greatest; highest

sumptus, -ūs (m.) expenditure

super (+ acc.) over

superbus, -a, -um haughty, proud, arrogant

superī, -ōrum (m. pl.) those inhabiting the heavens, the heavenly deities

superiniciō, -ere, -iniēcī, -iniectum to throw over a surface

superstes, -itis surviving after death

supersum, -esse, -fuī -futūrus to remain, be left over

supīnus, -a, -um turned palm upwards

suppleō, -ēre, -ēvī, -ētum to fill up

surgō, -ere, surrexī, surrectum to rise up

surrigō, -ere, surrexī, surrectum to rise up

surripiō, -ere, -rripuī, -rreptum to steal

sūs, suis (m., f.) pig, sow

suscitō, -āre, -āvī, -ātum to rouse, restore

suspendium, -ī (n.) hanging

suspendō, -ere, -ī, -pensum to hang, suspend

sustineō, -ēre, -uī to endure, tolerate

~suus, -a, -um his, her, its, their

# T

~tabella, -ae (f.) writing tablet

tābescō, -ere, tābuī to melt gradually

tabula, -ae (f.) account book

tacitus, -a, -um silent, quiet

taeda, -ae (f.) torch made of pine wood

tālis, -e such

tam (adv.) so, so very

~tamen (adv.) nevertheless

tamquam (conj.) as if

tandem (adv.) at last, finally

~tangō, -ere, tetigī, tactum to touch, come in contact with

tantum (adv.) only, merely, just; tantum ... quantum just so far ... as

tantus, -a, -um so great, such a great

tardē (adv.) slowly

tardus, -a, -um slow-moving

tectum, -ī (n.) roof, ceiling; house

tectus, -a, -um covered with a roof, roofed

tegō, -ere, texī, tectum to cover, conceal

tellūs, -ūris (f.) land, country

telum, -ī (n.) weapon, shaft

temerārius, -a, -um reckless, thoughtless, rash

Tempē (n. pl.) (indecl.) a valley known for its pastoral beauty at the foot of Mt. Olympus

temperō, -āre, -āvī, -ātum to moderate, regulate

templum, -ī (n.) temple

~temptō, -āre, -āvī, -ātum to try, attempt; to handle, touch, feel

tempus, -oris (n.) time; temple of the forehead

tenebrae, -ārum (f. pl.) darkness

Tenedos, -ī (f.) an island sacred to Apollo in the Aegean Sea

~teneō, -ēre, -uī, -tum to have, hold, preserve; to catch

tener, -era, -erum tender, sensitive; fragile

tenuis, -e fine, thin, tender

tepeō, -ēre to be warm, tepid

tepidus, -a, -um warm

ter (adv.) three times

teres, -etis smooth, rounded

tergeō, -ēre, tersī, tersum to wipe clean

tergum, -ī (n.) back

tergus, -oris (n.) back of an animal

terra, -ae (f.) earth, ground

tertius, -a, -um third

testa, -ae (f.) a fragment of earthenware

textum, -ī (n.) woven fabric, cloth

thalamus, -ī (m.) bedroom, marriage chamber

Thisbē, -ēs (f.) Thisbe

Thrēicius, -a, -um Thracian

Thynēius, -a, -um of or pertaining to the region of Bithynia

thyrsus, -ī (m.) a wand, usually covered with vine leaves, and carried by worshippers of Bacchus

tignum, -ī (n.) timber, rafter

tilia, -ae (f.) the lime (linden) tree

timeō, -ēre, -uī to fear, be afraid

~timidus, -a, -um fearful, apprehensive, timid

timor, -ōris (m.) fear, dread

tingō (tinguō), -ere, -nxī, -nctum to wet, soak; to dye, stain

tollō, -ere, sustulī, sublātum to pick up; to raise up

torpor, -ōris (m.) numbness, heaviness

torus, -ī (m.) cushion, bed

tot (indecl.) so many

totiens (adv.) so often

~tōtus, -a, -um the whole of

tractō, -āre, -āvī, -ātum to handle, manage

trādō, -ere, -idī, -itum to deliver, hand over

trahō, -ere, traxī, tractum to drag, draw; to influence

trāiciō, -ere, -iēcī, -iectum to transfix, pierce

transeō, -īre, -īvī, -itum to cross, pass through

transitus, -ūs (m.) passage

tremebundus, -a, -um trembling, quivering

tremō, -ere, -uī to tremble

tremulus, -a, -um quivering, shaking

trepidō, -āre, -āvī, -ātum to tremble, throb, quiver

tristis, -e unfriendly, dismal, sorrowful

triumphus, -ī (m.) the procession held in Rome to honor a victorious general

trivium, -ī (n.) crossroad, meeting point of three roads

Trōs, -ōis (m.) Trojan

truncō, -āre, -āvī, -ātum to strip off foliage

truncus, -ī (m.) a trunk

~tū you (sing.)

tueor, -ērī, tuitus to observe, watch over, guard

tum (adv.) then, at that moment

tumidus, -a, -um swollen, swelling

tumulō, -āre, -āvī, -ātum to entomb

tumulus, -ī (m.) grave

turba, -ae (f.) crowd of followers, attendants, troop

turbō, -inis (m.) whirlwind
turpis, -e loathsome, repulsive, shameful
tūs, tūris (n.) incense
tūtēla, -ae (f.) guardian, protection
tūtus, -a, -um safe, secure
~tuus, -a, -um your (sing.)

# U

ūber, -eris plentiful, abundant
ubi (adv.) where, when
ubīque (adv.) everywhere, anywhere
ullus, -a, -um any
ultimus, -a, -um final, last
ultrā (adv.) further, beyond that point
ulva, -ae (f.) rush, marsh grass
umbra, -ae (f.) shade, darkness, shadow
umbrōsus, -a, -um shady
umerus, -ī (m.) shoulder
umquam (adv.) never, ever (with nec)
ūnā (adv.) at the same time
~unda, -ae (f.) body of flowing water, river; water
undēnī, -ae, -a eleven at a time
ūnicus, -a, -um one, only one
~ūnus, -a, -um one; alone
urbs, -is (f.) city
urna, -ae (f.) urn
ūrō, -ere, ussī, ustum to burn, inflame with passion
usque (adv.) all the way
usus, -ūs (m.) use, purpose
~ut (conj.) just as, like; when; in order that; since
uterque, utraque, utrumque each, each . . . of the two
ūtilis, -e useful
ūtor, ūtī, ūsus (+ abl.) to make use of
ūva, -ae (f.) a bunch of grapes, grape
uxor, -ōris (f.) wife

# V

vacō, -āre, -āvī, -ātum to be empty, unfilled, vacant
~vacuus, -a, -um empty, unattached, free, unoccupied
vadimōnium, -ī (n.) a legal term referring to a guarantee that the parties in a suit will appear before the court at an agreed upon date and time

vagus, -a, -um shifting, moving about
valē, valēte farewell! good-bye!
vānus, -a, -um unreliable
vārus, -a, -um bent outward
vātēs, -is (m.) poet, prophet
-ve (conj.) or
vehō, -ere, vexī, vectum to carry
~vel (conj.) either . . . or; at any rate
vēlāmen, -minis (n.) garment, veil
vellō, -ere, vulsī, -sum to pull up
vēlō, -āre, -āvī, -ātum to cover
vēlox, -ōcis swift, speedy
velut (adv.) just as, just like, in the same way that
vēna, -ae (f.) blood vessel, vein
venia, -ae (f.) justification, excuse, indulgence
~veniō, -īre, vēnī, ventum to come
venter, -tris (m.) belly
ventilō, -āre, -āvī, -ātum to fan, brandish
ventus, -ī (m.) wind
Venus, -eris (f.) Venus, goddess sacred to love and lovers
~verbum, -ī (n.) word
vērē (adv.) truly, indeed
verēcundus, -a, -um modest
vereor, -ērī, -itus to be afraid
Vergilius, -ī (m.) Vergil
vērō (adv.) truly, really
Vērōna, -ae (f.) the city Verona in the north of Italy
verrō, -ere, versum to pass over, skim, sweep; to row
versō, -āre, -āvī, -ātum to turn
versus, -ūs (m.) a line of verse or writing
vertex, -icis (m.) the top of the head
vertō, -ere, -tī, -sum to turn into, change
verum (conj.) but
vērus, -a, -um real, genuine
vester, -tra, -trum your (pl.)
vestīgium, -ī (n.) footprint, sole of a foot, track
~vestis, -is (f.) clothing; cloth
vetō, -āre, -uī, -itum to forbid, prohibit
vetus, -eris old, of a former time, ancient
via, -ae (f.) journey, march, way
viātor, -ōris (m.) traveller
vibrō, -āre, -āvī, -ātum to wave, flutter

vīcīnia, -ae (f.) proximity

vīcīnus, -a, -um neighboring, close by

vicis (f.) (gen.) exchange, interaction; in vices by turns, alternately

victrix, -īcis victorious

victrix, -īcis (f.) victorious female

videō, -ēre, vīsī, vīsum to see, observe, gaze upon; to consider

vigil, -ilis (m.) sentry, guard

vīlis, -e worthless, common, ordinary

villa, -ae (f.) rural dwelling

vincō, -ere, vīcī, victum to defeat, conquer

vinculum, -ī (n.) chain, bond

vīnum, -ī (n.) wine

violentus, -a, -um violent, aggressive

vir, -ī (m.) man, husband

vireō, -ēre, -uī to sprout, show green growth

virgineus, -a, -um of or relating to a maiden, virgin

virginitās, -tātis (f.) maidenhood

~virgō, -inis (f.) maiden

vīs, vīs (f.) (pl.) strength

viscus, -eris (n.) innermost parts of the body

vīsō, -ere, -ī to view

vīta, -ae (f.) life

vitiō, -āre, -āvī, -ātum to impair, cause defects in

vītis, -is (f.) grapevine

vitium, -ī (n.) defect, fault; vice, moral failing

vītō, -āre, -āvī, -ātum to avoid

vitta, -ae (f.) headband

vīvō, -ere, vīxī, vīctum to live

vix (adv.) hardly, scarcely

vocō, -āre, -āvī, -ātum to call

volātus, -ūs (m.) flying, flight

volō, -āre, -āvī, -ātum to fly

~volō, velle, voluī to wish for; to wish

volucris, -cris (f.) bird

voluntās, -tātis (f.) willingness, intention

~vōs you (pl.)

vōtum, -ī (n.) vow, oath, prayer

vox, vōcis (f.) voice

vulgō, -āre, -āvī, -ātum to prostitute

vulgus, -ī (n.) general public, crowd, masses

~vulnus, -eris (n.) wound, injury

vultur, -uris (m.) vulture

vultus, -ūs (m.) facial expression; face

# AP* ANCILLARIES

## OVID VOCABULARY CARDS
### for AP* Selections
Richard A. LaFleur and Brad Tillery

Bound perforated cardstock vocabulary cards; unperforated cardstock (easy-assembly box, index, and grammatical forms summary) (2007), 8.5" x 11" Paperback, ISBN 978-086516-657-8

## OVID
### A LEGAMUS Transitional Reader
Caroline Perkins and Denise Davis-Henry

(2007), 8.5" x 11" Paperback, 978-0-86516-604-2

## THE LIVING VOICE OF LATIN
### Selections from Ovid
Stephen Daitz, read by Robert Sonkowsky

Booklet and two audio cassettes, 1-0005-2383-5

*AP is a registered trademark of the College Entrance Examination Board, which was not involved in the production of, and does not endorse, this product.

# OTHER OVID TITLES

## OVID *METAMORPHOSES*, Book 1
A. G. Lee

viii + 162 pp (1953, Reprinted 1988) 6" x 9" Paperback ISBN 978-0-86516-040-8

## OVID: Selections from ARS AMATORIA and REMEDIA AMORIS
Graves Haydon Thompson

168 pp. + fold-out (1952, corrected 1958, sixteenth reprint 1997)
6" x 9" Paperback, ISBN 978-0-86516-395-9

## OVID WITH LOVE
### Selections from ARS AMATORIA, Books I and II
Paul Murgatroyd

x + 228 pp. (1982, Reprint 1990) Paperback, ISBN 978-0-86516-015-6

 **BOLCHAZY-CARDUCCI PUBLISHERS, INC.**
### www.BOLCHAZY.com